T0319902

Borderland Anxieties

Asian Borderlands

This series presents the latest research on borderlands in Asia as well as on the borderlands of Asia – the regions linking Asia with Africa, Europe and Oceania. Its approach is broad: it covers the entire range of the social sciences and humanities. The series explores the social, cultural, geographic, economic and historical dimensions of border-making by states, local communities and flows of goods, people and ideas. It considers territorial borderlands at various scales (national as well as supra- and sub-national) and in various forms (land borders, maritime borders) but also presents research on social borderlands resulting from border-making that may not be territorially fixed, for example linguistic or diasporic communities.

Series Editors:
Willem van Schendel, University of Amsterdam
Tina Harris, University of Amsterdam

Editorial Board:
Franck Billé, University of California Berkeley
Eric Tagliacozzo, Cornell University
Yuk Wah Chan, City University Hong Kong
Duncan McDuie-Ra, University of New South Wales

Borderland Anxieties

Shifting Understandings of Gender, Place and Identity at the India-Burma Border

Matthew Wilkinson

Amsterdam University Press

Cover illustration: Matthew Wilkinson

Cover design: Coördesign, Leiden
Lay-out: Crius Group, Hulshout

ISBN	978 94 6372 978 9
e-ISBN	978 90 4855 703 5 (pdf)
DOI	10.5117/9789463729789
NUR	756

Every effort has been made to obtain permission to use all copyrighted illustrations reproduced in this book. Nonetheless, whosoever believes to have rights to this material is advised to contact the publisher.

Printed and bound by CPI Group (UK) Ltd, Croydon, CR0 4YY

Table of Contents

Acknowledgements

Producing this book has been an immense undertaking. A number of people have lent me their time and energy while writing this. First and foremost, an immense thanks to my supervisor, Professor Duncan McDuie-Ra. Your work and your words have encouraged my initial journeys to Nagaland and have been a constant boost to my own confidence. This book would not exist without your input, guidance, and friendship. Second, thank you Dr. Tanya Jakimow for the hours you have spent thoroughly reading my work, and your detailed feedback and support. Your input has moulded this book into a more coherent whole and has greatly improved my own writing. Thank you also to Dr. Dolly Kikon. Dolly, your work with women in Nagaland was the initial inspiration for this book, and as I spoke with men in Nagaland I hoped that I was doing justice to your efforts exploring gender, society, and culture in Nagaland. Dr. Xonxoi Barbora, your support and friendship have been constant since my initial field trip. Thank you also to Monalisa Changkija, you took me in as a scrappy grad student, fed me and encouraged me to never stop digging, and I remember our long conversations fondly. Dr. Nicholas Apoifis, you taught me to be bolder and braver in my writing. Thank you as well to some key academics, friends, and colleagues who have helped me along the way. These people have lent me their thoughts, opinions, and in many cases have put food in my stomach and a roof over my head – Professor Kama Maclean, Dr. Susanne Schmeidl, Dr. Anwesha Dutta, Dr. Michael Heneise, Dr. Fengshi Wu, Dr. Colin Clark, Mrs. Rita Kutchevskis-Hayes, Dr. Dominic Fitzsimmons, The mysterious Samson Thurr. Thank you also to the North East Social Research Centre in Guwahati, and the Don Bosco Centre at Karghuli, for giving me a space to work and sleep as I wrote. An immense *tike ase, moi bishi kuchi paishei* to my close friends in Nagaland and in Assam. For reasons of privacy I won't name all of you here, but if we drank at Quaff, Pebbles, BullyBar, Blacksheep or any of Dimapur's other shady nightclubs, you know who you are. You've let me into your homes and into your lives as I have written this, and this book is a product of the start, not the end, of our adventures together.

Part 1

Periphery

1   'The Nagaland State Co-operative Bank Ltd. Welcome You to Nagaland'

Abstract

Chapter 1 discusses the background of the research that led to the book, and offers an introduction to Nagaland as a frontier and borderland. The chapter also offers a discussion of borderlands, anxiety, and the role of gender in borderlands, and discusses the methodology and methodological considerations of the book.

Keywords: borderland, frontier, anxiety, gender.

The thoughts that shaped this book began in their haziest sense in 2012, when I was travelling through Bangladesh on a personal mission to reach and explore the Chittagong Hill Tracts in the country's east – three hilly districts that have witnessed decades of communal violence between migrant Bengali settlers from the plains and tribal communities indigenous to the hills. After several months in Bangladesh, I travelled overland through the Dawki Border gate to the Indian state of Meghalaya, and then to the state of Assam, a lowland valley state bordered by six highland 'tribal states' – Meghalaya, Tripura, Mizoram, Manipur, Arunachal Pradesh, and Nagaland, as well as the Kingdom of Bhutan. These 'tribal' states are home to distinct tribal communities, unique geography and complex politics similar to the communities, geography and politics that captured my interest in the Chittagong Hill Tracts. Following this interest, I took the six-hour Kamrup Express train from Assam into the state of Nagaland. My intention in coming to Nagaland was to travel from Kohima, the state capital, to the village of Longwa – a small hilltop settlement of around eighty thatch huts that is divided in two by the India/Burma border, in Mon District, Nagaland's most isolated and poorest district. The journey was an opportunity to engage with people living along the border and to continue to observe

Wilkinson, Matthew: *Borderland Anxieties. Shifting Understandings of Gender, Place and Identity at the India-Burma Border.* Amsterdam: Amsterdam University Press, 2023
DOI: 10.5117/9789463729789_CH01

the complexities of securitized governance, border politics, and armed conflict that have become the background to life at the borderlands between India, Myanmar and Bangladesh.

Arriving at Nagaland's largest city, Dimapur, after midnight, I was confronted with a rusty, muddy, foothills town not dissimilar to the towns I had visited in Assam. The kilometres leading up to the station were crowded with corrugated iron sheds and bamboo shacks along the railway tracks. Dimapur station itself was built in the same utilitarian style as the stations in neighbouring Assam, with a rusted tin roof hanging over the platform and grey floor tiles spattered with occasional stains from paan spit – a popular mix of betel leaf, areca nut, spices, and tobacco that is chewed and stains teeth and saliva a distinct dark red, which is then spat out. However, some differences quickly became apparent. As a foreigner, I was required to immediately register at the police headquarters located at the train station. Inside the smoky, sunken concrete station, while swatting mosquitos and speaking over the noise of trains outside, Khaki-uniformed Dimapur police questioned at length about my reasons for coming to Nagaland, how long I planned to stay, where I would be staying, and who I would be staying with. As one officer questioned me, another furiously jotted my answers into a logbook. When the officers were satisfied and I was allowed to leave the station, I encountered a group of Nagaland Armed Police (NAP) officers standing in the attached parking lot with automatic rifles in hand, their brown camouflage uniforms distinguishing them from the local police inside the station. A few hundred metres ahead, a fog-light-lit pillbox built onto the parking lot's perimeter wall overlooked the station and parking lot. The camouflage netting draped over the pillbox served to make the structure more conspicuous and imposing rather than conceal it. Immediately next to the pillbox a large sign read 'The Nagaland State Co-operative Bank Ltd. Welcome You to Nagaland'.

Nagaland was formed in 1963 as India's sixteenth state, bound by the Indian states of Assam to the west, Arunachal Pradesh to the north, Manipur to the south, and India's border with Myanmar to the east. The state is home to approximately 2.2 million people (Government of India, 2011). Tribal communities constitute 86.5 per cent of this population, almost all being from 17 Naga tribes.[1] The remaining 13.5 per cent includes a large community

---

1   Tribal recognition in Nagaland is contentious. Recognition of a distinct tribe brings with it rights over land and resources, political recognition, and the possibility of special reservations in lucrative public jobs. The number of tribes and what constitutes a 'Naga' tribe is an unsettled

Figure 1: 'Nagaland State Co-operative Ltd. Welcome you to Nagaland'.
Dimapur. 2016. Taken by author.

of Marwari traders who migrated to Nagaland during the 19th century, and more recent migrants from Assam, Bengal, Bihar, Nepal, Bhutan, and Bangladesh. In contrast to the established Hindu and Muslim populations in the Assam plains and other parts of India, over 90 per cent of the state's population identify as Christian (Government of India, 2011). In terms of GDP, Nagaland is one of India's poorer states. The state economy is primarily agricultural. Livelihood options typically involve working on smallholder and household farms, informal resource extraction operations such as roadside

issue. Some scholars recognize over sixty-five distinct Naga tribes on either side of the India/ Myanmar border (Shimray, 2007; Tohring, 2010). India's 1991 Census recognizes thirty-five Naga tribes, including seventeen in Nagaland, fifteen in Manipur, and three in Arunachal Pradesh (Shimray, 2007). The Government of Nagaland Department of Personnel and Administrative Reforms (2016a) recognizes fourteen Naga tribes in Nagaland, as well as four non-Naga tribes who reside in Nagaland.

coal mining, working for and with insurgent groups, drawing income from smuggling alcohol – which has been illegal in Nagaland since 1989 – and working in precarious day-jobs as labourers or short-term hires. The state is divided into sixteen administrative districts, each of which has a corresponding-ly named township. In the state's west, are the districts of Dimapur – the only 'lowland' or plains district in Nagaland, Kohima – the state capital and political centre of Nagaland, and the districts Peren, Chümoukedima, Niuland, Wokha and Mokokchung. These western districts are much more developed, with tarred roads, hospitals and specialist clinics, schools, and relatively reliable electricity supplies. Nagaland's eastern districts of Tseminyü, Zunheboto, Phek, Kiphire, Shamator, Noklak, Tuensang, and Mon, often referred to as the 'interior districts', are very different. Infrastructure in these eastern districts is typically sparse and poorly maintained. Com-munications technologies such as phone networks are rudimentary and unreliable. Hospitals and clinics are less common and poorly resourced. There are fewer commercial buildings, and apart from subsistence farming or small-scale logging and mining operations, very few livelihood options. In these areas the state's presence is visibly thinned, with less police and fewer government services. The few government buildings that are present in these areas are often unattended and in a state of disrepair.

Tense experiences such as the interactions described above – of rigid and anxious bureaucratic processes, engaging with police when moving between places, and of being under the watch of armed forces – are legacies of decades of armed conflict in Nagaland. This conflict centres on Nagaland's complex relationship with India. Before India's 1947 Independence, Nagaland, then the Naga Hills District, was a loosely mapped highland territory included as a part of Assam in British India. The District was granted special status under a succession of British policies allowing an ad hoc manner of governance, preserving local customary political institutions, and restricting migration into and out of the District. In the decades leading up to and following India's Independence, and citing this history of differential treatment and cultural, linguistic, and religious differences between Naga communities and other communities in India, Naga representatives sought to secure independent sovereignty for the Naga Hills. These calls were rejected by the Government of India, beginning a decades-long fight for independence in the Naga Hills. From the 1950s, India's paramilitary wing, the Assam Rifles, were stationed in the Naga Hills in efforts to subdue and control subversive groups in the District. An emergency law, the Armed Forces Special Powers Act (AFSPA) (1958), was drafted based on British-era anti-independence laws granting Indian paramilitaries extreme discretion and practical impunity in their treatment of Naga communities. With the impunities granted by AFSPA human rights abuses including summary executions, rape and other acts of sexual violence were committed widely and openly by Indian paramilitaries, especially in Nagaland's more isolated rural areas (Human Rights Watch, 2008). Village clearing and efforts to 'starve out' communities by burning crops and destroying grain stores were conducted, forcing many communities to live in hiding in Nagaland's jungles, eating scraps and drinking dirty water, in some cases for years (Iralu, 2009). Some discussants in rural areas reported witnessing beheadings committed by Indian paramilitaries during this period.[2] As the state's conflict dragged on, the Naga nationalist movement, once united in its efforts to resist Indian incursion, divided along ideological, tribal, and family lines. By the 1980s and 1990s, Naga communities found themselves caught between Indian paramilitaries targeting suspected guerrilla fighters in urban and rural areas on the one side, and various Naga insurgent groups targeting suspected spies and traitors within the Naga community while also making overlapping demands for donations, support, and shelter with threats of violence, on the other. While record-keeping was barely existent throughout the state's conflict, some estimates suggest 200,000 civilian and combatant deaths have occurred in Nagaland due to conflict since 1947 (Phillips, 2004).

This conflict is being brought to a close, albeit slowly and with many interruptions. In 1997 and 2001, two ceasefires were signed between the Government of India and Nagaland's two largest nationalist groups, the National Socialist Council of Nagaland – Isak-Muivah (NSCN-IM) and the National Socialist Council of Nagaland – Khaplang (NSCN-K) respectively. Since ceasefire, Nagaland has been in a tense and prolonged peace-conflict continuum. Open hostility between Naga nationalist groups and the Indian state has officially ended, although ceasefires are occasionally broken or abandoned. Various Naga nationalist groups, town guards, village vigilantes and breakaway factions within nationalist groups fight each other in a decades-long turf war for control over key territories and transport routes to extort a conflict-tired Naga public. Various political groups in Nagaland and in neighbouring states including the Nagaland State Government and the state governments of Assam and Manipur, reject and contest Nagaland's current borders, and police from these states occasionally fight each other across state borders (Agrawal and Kumar, 2017). Adding to the state's border complications, several Naga nationalist groups

2   This was raised in discussions in 2012 and followed up in 2016. The villages that these claims were made in and about were corroborated but are not named in this book for reasons of confidentiality and security.

endorse an alternative map of the state entirely, *Nagalim,* which includes Nagaland's current borders and also encompasses Naga inhabited areas in neighbouring Arunachal Pradesh, Assam, Manipur, and Myanmar (Baruah, 2007). In the midst of these contestations and tensions, the AFSPA continues to be applied and Naga civilians continue to be killed by Indian paramilitaries in real, mistaken, and staged encounters.

Travel in Nagaland is slow and arduous. Civilian infrastructure and service provision by the state government stagnated during decades of armed conflict, especially in the state's rural and interior areas. Roads are typically poorly maintained and bridges often collapse, leaving many towns and villages cut off. Indian paramilitaries and the Nagaland State Police regularly hold stop-and-checks at town entries, where private vehicles, public buses and commercial trucks are searched for arms, drugs, alcohol, and where passengers are required to produce identification documents. Arriving at a town or village often involves having details checked and recorded by local authorities and sometimes being questioned about previous movements and the reasons for coming to or passing through the town or village. On entering a town, it was sometimes a matter of minutes before a Nagaland Armed Police officer would stop and escort me to a damp station or office to fill a worn-out logbook with my name, visa details, and any other information officers felt could be relevant at that moment. The reasons for these stringent security procedures were rarely explained, but questions about the necessity of procedures were often met with vague references to the state being dangerous, sensitive, or simply because those were the rules that had to be followed. Owing to these difficulties, and due to the state's reputation as unstable and dangerous, foreign tourists have only recently made inroads into Nagaland. Tourists tend to restrict their visits to Dimapur and Kohima. Some tourists travel to Mon district in the north, although due to the state of the roads and the politically unsettled nature of the northern parts of the state, the numbers are very small. With the exception of Mon, foreign visitors rarely come to Nagaland's more isolated 'interior' territories. For this reason, my arrival in many towns and villages was met with excitement and fanfare. People were eager to ask where I had come from, how I had come to Nagaland, and what I was doing in their town. I was often invited to eat and sometimes stay in people's homes. These were people that I had met on long distance bus rides and had gotten to know sitting and talking with, or sometimes were people who had seen me in their town, noticed that I was foreign and invited me to share a meal. In some cases, people in one town had phoned ahead to the next town to announce the foreigner en-route, and I was met on arrival by the relatives and friends of previous encounters.

Through time spent in towns and villages, conversations on long rides in Nagaland State Transport (NST) buses, and meals shared throughout the state, a complex picture of life in Nagaland emerged. This differed between age groups, genders, urban and rural residents, but common themes were apparent. First, Nagaland appeared to embody imaginings of 'remoteness', 'isolation', and 'backwardness' yet simultaneously seemed to be of immense importance to the Government of India. This remoteness, isolation, and a sense of being 'left-behind' was manifest in the poor state of Nagaland's roads and infrastructure, the chronic under-funding of essential services such as health care and education, and a widely shared belief that Indian administrators looked the other way when it came to issues such as endemic corruption in the state's governance. Remoteness and 'backwardness' were often directly mentioned by discussants, with many people asking why I had come to such a 'backward place'. Yet, simultaneously, Nagaland is a focal point in India's efforts to securitize and promote 'peace through development' throughout Northeast India (Chasie and Hazarika, 2009). The state has one of the highest proportions of police and armed force per capita in the country (Parliament of India, 2022), and various paramilitary outfits maintain a permanent presence that involves well maintained and expansive camps that resemble small, self-contained cities. Besides these security imperatives, Nagaland is increasingly connected to other parts of India, other parts of Asia, and to overseas through resource extraction projects (Kikon, 2019), the very active Baptist church in the state (Longkumer, 2018), a burgeoning tourism industry (Longkumer, 2013), new connective technologies (Yimchunger, 2020), and a growing Naga diaspora (Angelova, 2015). Essentially, Nagaland seemed be very peripheral and isolated yet very central and connected, simultaneously, and in ways that seemed to contradict each other.

Second, disparities between younger and older Nagas were notable. This was especially the case in the ways younger and older Nagas discussed their opinions on the state's security situation and future as a part of India. The older people that I spoke with – people in their fifties, sixties, seventies, and occasionally eighties – regaled me with stories of Nagaland's long fight for independence. They discussed, often in gruesome detail, atrocities committed by Indian paramilitaries. They gave accounts of widespread village burning, summary executions, and of having to hide and live in Nagaland's dense forests, forage for food after dark, and drink dirty water. Some gave first-hand accounts of being tortured by Indian paramilitaries. Occasionally, older Nagas mentioned being members of or knowing members of Naga nationalist groups such as the Naga National Council (NNC) and Naga Federal Government (NFG), often using the term 'freedom fighters' when discussing these groups. Older people were more likely to speak positively about the Naga nationalist movement, and often espoused their support for an independent sovereign Nagaland, an expansive Naga homeland referred to as 'Nagalim', with its own borders extending into Naga inhabited territories in the neighbouring states of Arunachal Pradesh, Assam, Manipur, and including a large part of Myanmar. Younger people – in their teens, twenties, thirties, and forties – while often aware of Nagaland's conflict and sharing some knowledge of injustices committed during the conflict, were much more focused on problems finding work in Nagaland and of corruption and poor governance throughout the state. While some younger people expressed support for Naga autonomy, most were also critical of the overlapping taxation systems violently enforced by multiple nationalist groups. For young people I spoke with living in Nagaland's larger urban centres, Naga independence was viewed as antithetical to the state's development and to their own futures, although young urban residents also criticized India's armed presence in the state and the atrocities associated with militarization. Younger Nagas often mentioned the opportunities that greater connections to India brought, and discussed their own intentions to travel, study, or find work outside of Nagaland in larger Indian cities, far away from Nagaland. Many of the contacts I made have followed through with those intentions and have moved to other Indian cities such as Delhi and Bangalore.

Finally, gender was a recurring issue in many of these discussions. Gender appeared in discussions of the state's future and in discussions about the difference between Naga culture and a roughly framed pan-Indian culture from the plains. In many cases, gender roles, alongside religion, were presented as key distinguishing factors of Naga society and identity. Many discussants, younger and older, made a special point that women's freedoms surrounding work and the absence of arranged marriages and dowry in Naga culture (although arranged marriages do take place in some Naga families) were indicative of Naga culture being 'more modern' and more egalitarian than cultures based in the Indian plains. However, often in these same conversations, discussants mentioned that Naga women lacked a 'strength' required to be household and community leaders, that Naga women should not be involved in the state's politics and should not have the right to own ancestral land. These discussions almost always took place in groups of men without women present. These views were common across a range of age groups but for different reasons. Older Nagas tended to discuss the moral decay brought by young people, especially by women, leaving towns and villages and pursuing urban livelihoods in other parts of India. Younger Nagas, especially younger men, tended to discuss the personal risks and wider societal disruption associated with Naga women becoming involved with men who were not Nagas, especially Bangladeshi migrants and 'Miyas'.[3] There was a general consensus across age groups that there once existed a natural gendered balance in Naga society, and that this balance was being upset by women's newfound agency in workplaces, greater ability to travel independently, women's romantic involvement with non-Nagas, and women's agitations for political and land-ownership rights. These were issues that discussants implicitly presented as having emerged since ceasefire or having become more common since ceasefire.

Gender in Nagaland is explored in-depth by a number of scholars. In particular, discussions focus on women's victimization by Indian paramilitaries and laws of exception (Gill, 2005; Iralu, 2017); gendered and sexual violence within the Naga community (Kikon, 2015; North East Network, 2016); and women's roles as peacemakers between armed forces and nationalist groups during the conflict (Manchanda, 2004, 2005; Manchanda and Bose, 2011). This focus is warranted. Naga society is patriarchal. Deeply engrained patriarchal norms exist in the administration of state governance, in customary institutions, and at the household level. These patriarchal norms, of men as leaders and as associated with the public sphere, and of women as followers of their fathers or husbands and associated with the private sphere, are argued by many Nagas as fundamental aspects of Naga culture and identity. Conflict in Nagaland is also highly gendered. Militarization involves the encroachment of a hyper-masculine nationalistic military occupation in the form of male soldiers from far away who act with impunity and are above the law. The Naga nationalist struggle also involved the emergence and promotion of a hyper-masculine Naga nationalist movement that stood at odds with the occupying Indian hegemon and reified men's self-styled roles as guardians and protectors. Even as the conflict is being brought to a close and this nationalist movement loses much of its popular support, the hyper-masculine political culture it has encouraged continues, dominated by 'strongmen' politicians and community leaders who channel guardian and protector roles (Wouters, 2018). In light of the state's rigidly patriarchal structures, Naga men are often discussed as being hyper-conservative, xenophobic and as inextricably tied to archaic and patriarchal customary

3   'Miya' originally referred to the 'Miya' Muslim peasant community that settled in Assam in the 19th century, but now is often used to refer broadly to dark-skinned Indians from the plains living in Nagaland. Miya is often used to refer to the Marwari traders who have been settled in Nagaland since the 19th century, migrants from other parts of India, especially Bihar, and Bangladeshi migrants.

traditions. These understandings are present in academic literature and are also widely accepted in the Naga community. When reflecting on discussions with relatives and other Naga women about sexual violence in the state, Kikon (2015: 70) mentions some of the ways these connections are constructed in the Naga community:

> I remember many instances when aunties and well-respected Naga women, along with their husbands and sons, would justify all kinds of violence against women by saying 'but it is the trait of a Naga man to be like this. We have to adjust and forgive them'. Such justification and naturalization of violence as part of Naga culture, compounded by a colonial framework that continues to define Naga men as 'fierce warriors', 'hot headed men', or 'blood thirsty people' must be interrogated. However, at times, it appears that we accept this violent construction as the foundation of our values and morality; as though Naga identity, being a Naga, the core of our Naganess is built on violence, disrespect towards the young and vulnerable, and a culture where the rich and powerful get away with everything.

However, these discussions and observations, and the tensions they illustrate obscure a number of important dynamics that are relevant in the state's politics and are tied to conflict, gender, and the experience of living in a peripheral borderland. First, ceasefires have encouraged a reconfiguration of relationships between Naga communities and the Indian centre. This is a slow process, one that is marked by interruptions and exceptions but is ongoing and is accelerating, nonetheless. As the disruptions of armed conflict become less common, new markets and opportunities are emerging, especially in Nagaland's growing urban hubs. The emergence of this post-conflict consumer economy is enabled by and contributes to the state's rapid urbanization. Young Nagas especially are leaving smaller towns and villages to move to Nagaland's larger urban hubs. As a part of this change, rigid patriarchal customs are questioned from within the Naga community in the form of increasing calls for inclusive governance by feminist Nagas, made more possible in the relative stability of ceasefire. Many of the village-based livelihood models that endorse rigidly gendered social norms, such as women as homemakers and submissive followers, and men as leaders and hunters, are waning. For many, these challenges are seen as chipping at the cornerstones of Naga society and identity. Second, Naga nationalist groups have lost a great deal of relevance. Many of the associations between masculinity and nationalist insurgency have been severed as involvement in the 'underground' has become more closely associated with extortion and smuggling than with pushes for an independent Naga homeland. The criminal-turn of Naga nationalist groups from freedom fighters to extortionists has left many current and former Naga nationalist workers at the margins of a changing society and economy, further exacerbating the associations between insurgency and irrelevance in the post-conflict society. Hence, there is a growing divide between the 'old' push for independent sovereignty, and the newfound benefits of closer engagements with the Indian centre. Finally, migration into and out of the state is accelerating. Nagas are leaving the state in great numbers in search of work, education, and to live away from a changing but still relatively poor and isolated borderland state of India. Simultaneously, migrants from other parts of India, Bangladesh, Nepal, and from overseas come to Nagaland for many of the opportunities presented by the state's growing post-conflict economy. The intermingling of outsiders and Nagas creates tensions and anxieties surrounding the survival of a cohesive Naga identity, as many Nagas fear a wave of outsiders are coming to take over the state. Gender plays a central role in all of the above dynamics. The gendered manifestations of change in Nagaland are subtle and often enmeshed with other social and political issues, but are significant nonetheless. Exploring these dynamics in Nagaland offers rich insights into the ways anxieties associated with sovereignty, culture and territory are manifest in everyday debates about gender and identity in borderlands.

Borderlands, Anxiety, Gender

Throughout this book I discuss the ways that anxieties associated with Nagaland's borders shape gendered politics in the wake of decades of armed conflict in the state. 'Border' suggests a rigid and clear separation between states, populations, economies, and cultures. Cartographic lines present a territorial vision of the state as having distinct zones of control and authority. Through the use of border guards, customs officials, armies and paramilitaries, fortifications, fences and gates, this territorial vision is violently enforced. Agamben (2005) employs the metaphor of the 'camp' to illustrate the ways this enforcement takes place, arguing that borders and other sites that are subject to exceptional treatment are where the mechanisms of sovereignty and subject-making are displayed in their rawest forms. Populations in these sites are subject to a 'state of exception' where individual political rights are nullified and the individuals are reduced to a state of 'bare life' – stripped of their political rights and agency and recognized only through their bare biological existence (2005). At these sites the parameters of citizenship and belonging to the state are made real, and populations who are suspect, who live on or who live across the border are subjected *to* the state but not subjects *of* the state. Essentially, the border is imagined as static monument where the state's sovereignty abruptly begins and where the state's monopoly of violence is most clearly displayed.

While Agamben's (2005) approach is useful for framing the ways that borders and other sites create citizens with rights and non-citizens without rights, borders and borderlands are also far from static, fixed, or unchallenged. Conflict, militarization, extractive regimes, traditional and customary institutions, and differential property regimes meet, compete, and coalesce at and across borders (Rasmussen and Lund, 2018). Borders shift and change, requiring daily reproduction through practices of territorialization, access control, inclusion and exclusion (van Houtum and van Naerssen, 2002). Where states attempt to control movement and stamp their presence at the border, border communities, migrants, traders, refugees, smugglers, corrupt police and officials, armed forces and paramilitaries exploit and create opportunities that derail the state's mission. In some cases, these subversions are momentary and fleeting. When evading official border crossings, border-crossers, momentarily, reject cumbersome and limiting bureaucratic processes (Jones, 2012). In others, these subversions may be profitable hustles that co-opt the state's often cumbersome bureaucratic processes. Through commandeering border gates and access routes, customs officials create their own modes of statehood and subversive economies as much for practicality as for their own personal gain, blurring the lines between the political state and personal enterprises (Chalfin, 2010). In other cases, these subversions challenge the state's claims to territory, and in some ways challenge the legitimacy of state itself. Various state-resistant and rebel groups take sanctuary across borders when in conflict with states, and borderlands offer valuable pools of support and resources for groups rejecting and resisting the state-making project (Brown, 2013). Communities at borders offer their own alternative border maps, rejecting those drawn by the state. Jurisdictions overlap, and local communities often find themselves living across multiple overlapping sovereign projects, including those of their own making (Dunn and Cons, 2014).

As states attempt to secure valuable resources and foster regional connections, borderlands have increasingly become targets of state-led liberalization projects with aims to build connective infrastructure, foster local economic development, and connect state margins to the centre (Eilenberg, 2014).

These efforts go hand-in-hand with ongoing exceptional legal treatment, militarization, and draconian enforcement of state structures and norms (Plonski and Yousuf, 2017). Through these overlaps, borderlands and the margins of the state witness dynamic and dramatic changes between order-making projects that produce overlapped, messy forms of sovereignty at local and global intersections. This is especially the case in Northeast India, where projects involving building and expanding infrastructure, exploiting natural resources and engaging with local economies are enmeshed in efforts of subduing state-resistance and are imbibed with a rhetoric of 'peace through development' (Sarmah, 2016). This makes borderlands, margins and other state peripheries valuable sites to witness the contested state-making project. Tsing (1993: 27) argues that

> turning to state peripheries shed[s] light on both the limitations and the strengths of state agendas. An out-of-the-way place is, by definition, a place where the instability of political meanings is easy to see. The authority of national policies is displaced through distance and the necessity of re-enactment at the margins. The cultural difference of the margins is a sign of exclusion from the centre; it is also a tool for destabilizing state authority.

The emergence of alternative sovereignties, or negotiated forms of sovereignty, produces new dynamics and politics, rendering borderlands sites of creative cultural production (Rosaldo, 1989: 208). Belcher et al. (2015) argue that 'borders do more than simply mark territorial margins … borders are epistemological and material sites with the power to shape subjectivities, differentiate and produce categories of "citizen" and "migrant", and trace inclusive and exclusive fields of possibilities, as well as limits'. Essentially, at borders new identities are formed and radical political subjectivities are forged'.

The border anxieties that I discuss are thus not limited to anxieties associated with Nagaland's international border with Burma, nor to Nagaland's border with the neighbouring state of Assam, nor Manipur, nor Arunachal Pradesh, all of which have been the subject of border disagreements and conflicts in recent history. Rather, the border anxieties I discuss in this book are a collection of dynamics associated with homelands, identity, and change that sometimes are relevant at the border, sometimes are relevant far away from the border, but nonetheless involve the border and encompass the idea of boundaries, 'insiders' and 'outsiders' in some way. Locally understood meanings of border are informed by and also inform myriad political and social dynamics that centre on defining distinct spaces and attaching populations, forms and norms to those spaces. This flexible conceptualization of 'border', as not just embodied in a mapped line or territorial space, but as subjective, overlapped and temporal, reflects the often layered and divergent ways that borders are imagined and discussed. In Nagaland, 'border' and loose references to borders were used to refer to various mapped, unmapped, real, and imagined dividing lines simultaneously. In public debates about migration, 'border' was used to refer to India's international border with Bangladesh, which is not in Nagaland, but also to Nagaland's state borders. References to dividing lines and an ambiguous boundary between Northeast India and the Indian 'centre' were used in discussions about governance and the legitimacy of the Indian state. Similar references to boundaries and borders were used when mentioning an amorphous gulf between tribal and non-tribal communities in Northeast India, usually in terms of foothills marking the dividing lines between 'highland' tribal communities and 'lowland' plains populations. This approach reflects that of Yuval-Davis, Wemyss and Cassidy's (2019: 18, 19) consideration of border-making and 'bordering' as taking place

> inside and outside, as well as along the official borders of the state ... state borders are marked as fixed linear contours that are usually recognized by international law and in international relations as marking the official edges of territory or space over which one single state has control – a naturalized "homeland". This hegemonic imaginary ... covers political, social, cultural and economic realities that are much more complex and less stable than official discourse would want us to believe and reflect global as well as regional and national power relations.

Essentially, I approach Nagaland's borders as focal points of contestations over identity, legitimacy and belonging in ways that have relevance far beyond the border itself.

State-making projects at borderlands enact, produce, and require various forms of violence, including gendered violence (Nayak and Suchland, 2006). Securitization, militarization, and conflict at borderlands adds to these gendered dynamics. Women at borderlands are subject to a 'frontier culture of violence' occurring at the intersections of 'militarization, race, ethnicity, tribe, exceptionalism, and suspect populations' (McDuie-Ra, 2012c: 323). State-led projects of drawing, enforcing, and protecting borders are loaded with masculine discourses of 'men's work' and heroic civilizing missions (Hogan and Pursell, 2008). For example, India's Border Roads Organisation

(BRO), an integral piece of the Indian Government's efforts to extend road access in India's frontiers and border areas, features the following quote from the Mirror Magazine from July 1975 (Government of India Border Roads Organisation, 2019):

> Let us not forget that roads in this difficult terrain have been built not only with mere cement and concrete, but also with the blood of men of the Border Roads Organisation of India. Many lost their lives for the cause of duty on the project. To these men, who always play with danger and laugh at death, duty comes first. These fallen heroes came from all parts of Mother India, to contribute their mite to the defence of their mother land and prosperity of their neighbours.

As well as sites of contested meaning-making, borderlands are increasingly witness to processes of liberalization, commodification and global flows. Processes of liberalization have profound effects on the ways people engage with the state (Weiss, 2005), the way state officials engage with the public (Chalfin, 2010), and on aspirations (Zabiliute, 2016), understandings of self (Mathur, 2010), and relationships between generations (Philip, 2018). Some research has shown that liberalization in borderlands is contested and involves selective processes of engagement and resistance (McDuie-Ra, 2016b). The ways liberalization shapes masculinities and men's roles in borderlands, however, is only beginning to be understood. Coming to a deeper understanding of how men imagine, engage with, and experience liberalization is important because these communities often host long-established patriarchal traditions and hyper-masculine cultures associated with borderland conflicts (Bijukumar, 2019; Faludi, 1991; Hokowhitu, 2012; McDuie-Ra, 2012c; Myrttinen, 2012).

Building on these understandings of borderlands as sites of sovereign claim and challenge, but also as productive sites of subjectivity and meaning making, I investigate the ways that interwoven geographies, actors, and dynamics in a post-conflict borderland shape gendered politics and gendered violence. Anxieties about sovereignty, territory, and identity shape politics at borderlands, and these anxieties in Nagaland are manifest in the form of a newfound prominence of gender and debates surrounding gender. These anxieties are diverse and often ambiguous. They are implicit and often identified only after iterative stages of observation, discussion, and exposure. I use anxiety to refer to a collectively embodied sense of precarity and agitation. Various iterations of 'anxiety' are employed when discussing similar collective experiences and perceptions of insecurity, marginality and oppression. Appadurai (2006) refers to an 'anxiety of incompleteness' when discussing ethnonationalism and ethnocide, where anxieties emerge due to the perceived threats that ethnic and cultural differences pose to a cohesive sense of national community. As Appadurai (2006: 7) argues, these anxieties are magnified by the pressures of globalization:

> Globalization exacerbates these uncertainties and produces new in-centives for cultural purification as more nations lose the illusion of national economic sovereignty or well-being … Large-scale violence is not simply the product of antagonistic identities but that violence itself is one of the ways in which the illusion of fixed and charged identities is produced, partly to allay the uncertainties about identity that global flows invariably produce. In this regard, Islamic fundamentalism, Christian fundamentalism, and many other local and regional forms of cultural fundamentalism may be seen as a part of an emerging repertoire of efforts to produce previously unrequired levels of certainty about social identity, values, survival and dignity.

Diverting from Appadurai's anxiety of incompleteness, Middleton (2013a) conceptualizes an 'anxious belonging' specific to the state's geographic and symbolic margins. Focusing on sub-nationalist agitations for a separate state of Gorkhaland in Darjeeling, Middleton describes how the Ghorka population, brought to the highland municipality by British colonial authori-ties, have become the majority ethnic population while historical lacking recognition as Indian subjects. This has encouraged an anxious politics culminating in a decades-long push for a separate state of Ghorkaland, within India. Anxious belonging, rather than being an anxiety of producing a cohesive national or ethnic identity, thus refers to the anxieties associated with not belonging to the national majority. This is especially relevant for Nagas and for other Northeast Indian tribal communities, who sit outside of a narrowly framed but widely understood image of Indian identity (Wouters and Subba, 2013). Anxiety has been used before in discussions of political violence in Nagaland. Wouters (2022) discusses anxiety in Nagaland over migrant inflows and resulting perceptions of ethnic pollution and emascula-tion as causes of the 2015 mob lynching of Syed Farid Khan in Dimapur.

   Appadurai (2006) and Middleton (2013a, 2013b) lay important founda-tions for discussing borderland anxieties. Appadurai's (2006) anxiety of incompleteness offers a valuable explanation for the violence of majorities and hegemonic populations towards small minorities and other vulnerable groups. The imagining of violence as a mode of producing certainty about the bounds of identity offers a way of understanding spectacular and extreme acts of violence between ethnic, national, and religious groups. Middleton's (2013a, 2013b) anxious belonging opens discussion of the ways anxiety shapes politics and violence at the state's margins. I offer a deviation to these approaches to anxiety. Appadurai (2006), Middleton (2013a, 2013b) and Wouters (2022) focus on anxiety as a source of massed, organized and frenzied episodes of violence against a perceived 'other'. In many cases this explanation rings true, where acts of genocide, or political agitation, or spectacular violence serve to reify ethnic, racial and ideological divides. However, I propose that arguments that political anxieties and their resulting violence are unifying are narrow and ignore important forms of division and conflict created in anxious political environments. For every genocide discussed by Appadurai, there are instances of resistance and opposition to massed violence (Palmer, 2014). For every homeland movement such as the Ghorka nationalist movement, there are crucial internal disagreements about representation, identity and control (Wilkinson, 2015). In Dimapur's 2015 lynching, Wouters' (2022) references to a singular 'fiery mob', albeit with a passing recognition that 'not all parts of the mob actually committed violence' (p. 4), overlooks the condemnation of the lynching throughout Nagaland in the days following (Kikon, 2015). My intention in this book is not to refute or disregard the arguments made about collective anxiety and violence, but rather to show that 'anxiety' as a political object of inquiry is dynamic, multifaceted, and divisive. In exploring the ways anxieties at borderlands are dynamic and multifaceted, I analyse the ways that anxieties reveal divisions and conflicts in the Naga community emerging from a number of changes taking place in the post-conflict borderland.

Ethnographic Research in Borderlands

This is an ethnographic research book. Ethnography is a qualitative method-ology that involves extended time spent in a place, engaging with, talking to, and observing people and events (Whitehead, 2005). Ethnography emerged from colonial anthropology as a method used to understand and document colonies and the frontiers of colonial empires (Fuller, 2016). Early works such as Mauss' seminal Manuel d'Ethnographie (1926) attest to this legacy, being 'intended for administrators or colonists who lack professional training' (Mauss, 1926: 6). In the post-colonial era, ethnographies have expanded dramatically, and ethnography has acquired a range of meanings, all of which are associated with qualitative inquiry (Hammersley, 2018). This rapid growth in the use of and reference to ethnography has contributed to a sense of drift and vagueness regarding what ethnography actually is. As Ingold (2014: 383–385) argues,

> Ethnography has become a term so overused, both in anthropology and in contingent disciplines, that is has lost much of its meaning ... there is the ethnographic encounter, ethnographic fieldwork, ethnographic method, ethnographic knowledge. There are ethnographic monographs and ethnographic films. And now we have ethnographic theory! Through all of this runs the ethnographer. Taking this as a primary dimension of identity, it would appear that everything the ethnographer turns his or her hand to is, prima facie, ethnographic.

This confusion regarding what ethnography involves can roughly be attributed to two factors. First, to assumptions that ethnography is a loose term for any form of qualitative inquiry. Second, because ethnography is qualitative, that ethnography is often a solution to any of the limitations or criticisms of quantitative social research.

Despite this conceptual elusiveness, there are some overarching principles common to ethnographic approaches. Whitehead (2004: 18) argues that ethnography includes both qualitative and quantitative methods; has ontological and epistemological properties; is the study of culture from both 'emic' and 'etic' perspectives; is greatly dependent on fieldwork; and is an 'open-ended emergent learning process, and not a rigid investigator-controlled experiment'. Similarly, Hammersley and Atkinson (2007: 3) summarize five 'features' common to ethnographic research: that ethnography studies people's actions and accounts in everyday contexts, rather than under conditions created by the researcher; data is gathered from a range of sources, where participant observation and/or relatively informal conversations are usually central; data collection is, for the most part, relatively unstructured; the focus is usually on a few cases, generally small scale to facilitate in-depth study; the analysis of data involves interpretation of the meanings, functions, and consequences of human actions and institutional practices. Schatz (2009: 6) argues that two themes are central to ethnographic research – immersion and sensibility, where immersion refers to time spend immersed 'in a community, a cohort, a locale, or a cluster of related subject positions' and sensibility refers to 'a sensibility that goes beyond face-to-face contact. It is an approach that cares – with the possible emotional engagement that implies – to glean the meanings that the people under study attribute to their social and political reality'. In other words, Schatz argues that ethnography involves a researcher immersing themselves in a place, and that researcher seeks to understand the social and political reality of that place through a deep and personal involvement in that social and political reality. In a similar vein, Jonsson (2014) refers to 'slow anthropology' as an ethnographic approach marked by repeated trips to a field site over a period of years and becoming closely engaged in people's lives, in ways that often blur the boundaries between being a researcher from the outside, and an adopted member of the community. Gearoid (2018: 62–68) elaborates on the concept of ethnographic immersion, arguing that there are three crucial aspects that allow the immersed ethnographer to make valuable insights. These are extended periods of time in the field, allowing the researcher to develop relationships and participate in the community; exposure to chance, allowing serendipitous encounters and unexpected events to take place; and the opportunity to experience, observe, and investigate change.

Post-conflict sites are notoriously difficult sites to conduct ethno-graphic research. Accessing post-conflict sites is not only complicated by the limitations of the state to provide adequate security and functional infrastructure, but also by risk-management policies at the university level. Before researchers encounter the difficulties of doing fieldwork in areas marked by conflict, unreliable services and poor infrastructure, researchers must overcome the restrictive and sometimes insurmountable obstacles posed by university regulations, institutional and ethics review boards, and insurer requirements. Once research policies and review boards are satisfied and researchers come to a field site, access issues are compounded by limited public and private sector development. Researchers may not easily be able to find clean drinking water, reliable electricity, accommoda-tion, transport, mobile phone access, or other essential services (Roll and Swenson, 2019: 247). These problems may be overcome, but are time- and energy-consuming, and distract from focused research activities. Access difficulties may encourage a 'capital city trap' – a bias where research is limited to better-serviced, safer, and more populated areas. Data quality is also affected in post-conflict contexts, as conflict and its legacies may often restrict the ability of the state and of other institutions to collect, store, and maintain data; as people are traumatized and may distrust researchers, and may either resist taking part in the research entirely or may provide limited, skewed, or false information; and where people may have poorer education and are less able to answer surveys, understand the purpose of the research, or are less able to distinguish time periods and places due to experiences of disruption and trauma (2019: 253). These challenges are magnified in post-conflict borderlands, where sensitivities surrounding the border often results in an omnipresent securitized nature to the state, ambiguity about where one can and cannot go, and the presence of black economies, legal, semi-legal and illegal cross-border economies and interactions (see van Schendel and Abraham, 2005).

Research in Nagaland exemplifies these challenges. Nagaland and several of its neighbouring states, including Assam and Manipur, are considered 'high-risk' locations by several governments. The US Department of State places Nagaland and six Northeast Indian states on a 'do not travel' list and bans embassy and consulate staff from entry without authorization from the US Consulate General in Kolkata. The UK Government's foreign travel advice is less restrictive, but mentions the December 2021 attack by Indian security forces on civilians in Nagaland as a reason to exercise caution. The Australian Government advises reconsidering all travel to Nagaland and its neighbouring states, as does the New Zealand Government, and the Irish Department of Foreign Affairs.[4] While not all governments take the same position, the widespread caution against travelling to Nagaland complicates research processes applied by university regulations, institutional and ethics review boards, and insurance providers. Physical access and movement in Nagaland is also complicated by changing bureaucratic requirements for foreign visitors. Before 2011, all foreign visitors in Nagaland were required to obtain an Inner Line Permit (ILP) to travel in Nagaland. These permits were a means to control and monitor access into Nagaland and restrict movement to particular parts of the state. While the Inner Line Permit (ILP) system was suspended between 2011 and 2019, police and other officials during that period were often unsure of registration requirements for foreigners and often expected foreigners to carry an ILP or other permit for travel in the area. This was especially the case in more isolated, interior towns and villages. In November 2019 the ILP system was reinstated for foreigners throughout Nagaland, making it much more difficult to conduct long research trips in the state. Where an ILP can be obtained, research can nevertheless be slowed and disrupted by confusion about changing bureaucratic requirements and inquiries by local authorities.

Living and working in Nagaland is also very disruptive. Bandhs and other strikes are occasionally called by local political groups, shutting down travel and commerce. If there is a suspicion of a bandh coming up, people will often hoard cash, bottled water and fuel, and this can slow movement and disrupt all activity in the state, research included. Prolonged

4   The above advice against travelling to Nagaland and other parts of Northeast India predates the Coronavirus pandemic.

periods of time spent in the state, especially for researchers who are not Indian, elicits curiosity and suspicion from security forces. The security imperatives that govern access to and movement in Nagaland encourage an environment where the movements of foreigners outside of the tourist season in December are closely watched by armed forces. The attention on foreign visitors means that many locals are wary of being seen speaking to foreign researchers. While less common than it was before ceasefire, being arrested, tortured, or disappearing at the hands of Indian paramilitaries or suspicious nationalist-insurgents is still a very real risk, one that is realized in everyday interactions with Indian paramilitaries and Naga nationalist groups. To quote a source in Nagaland, 'everybody has a story', often of an uncomfortable interaction with Indian paramilitaries, of somebody being temporarily detained, or forced to provide identification details, or otherwise delayed or inconvenienced by Indian paramilitaries. Many households also have stories of a relative or friend being a member or suspected member of a nationalist group or suspected of being a spy, having been arrested and questioned by either Indian paramilitaries or an insurgent gang, sometimes their own, and being beaten, killed, or disappearing completely. As well as fears of being detained or arrested by Indian paramilitaries or Naga insurgents, fears of other reprisals are also present when discussing any issues related to Naga nationalist groups. People are scared of offending pro-nationalists or of being misquoted as offending pro-nationalists. Reprisals may involve public shaming or social ostracism, or threatening a person's family members in other parts of the state. Because of this, many people in Nagaland are hesitant to discuss or of being suspected of discussing political or otherwise sensitive issues with outsiders.

Besides the difficulties presented by the state's security situation, recent changes to Nagaland's economy and accelerating migration flows further complicate the research process. People often move to different towns and different parts of towns for seasonal work, to assist with and care for family in other parts of the state, and during holidays and festival seasons. Many people spend long periods living in other parts of India entirely, and some move overseas. Mobile phone numbers are also often changed or are sold on to new users through India's expansive 'grey numbers' trade, where working phone numbers are sold on to second and third users to avoid tedious and time-consuming bureaucratic processes when registering a new phone number. For example, when initial fieldwork for this research began in January 2016, it had been nearly four years since my last visit to Nagaland, and while some of the people I had met on my first trip to Nagaland in 2012 were still reachable, most had moved away or had changed their phone numbers in the time since my earlier visit. I had compiled a list of the contact details and addresses of local government offices and NGOs that I had identified online, but this also proved to be of little use. Many of the addresses I had listed before my arrival had been replaced by new tenants or had been knocked down in the state's ongoing urban construction boom. This presented an immense challenge for the research process. I had begun fieldwork studying men and local understandings of masculinity with few, if any, local contacts. The challenge of finding people to interview was magnified by the legacies of decades of conflict in the state and ongoing tensions between the Naga public, Indian armed forces, and Naga nationalist groups.

To overcome these challenges, I read local newspapers and magazines and became a frequent visitor to several local newspaper offices. Being close to journalists especially gave me access to prominent local businesspeople, commentators, activists, and politicians. I visited several government offices and departments for the purposes of my own research and as company of several associates who wanted to expose me to the frustrations of bureaucracy in the state, and I suspect, also hoped bringing a foreign visitor would lend legitimacy to their inquiries and strengthen their cases. Throughout multiple field trips I became embedded in everyday life in Nagaland, learning rudimentary Nagamese, navigating the bureaucratic and social complexities of staying in Nagaland for prolonged periods and travelling in different parts of the state, and developing close associations and friendships. I stayed in cheap local hotels and dormitories. I lived with families and friends. I used public buses for short and long trips. I went to church on Sundays. I attended local debates and book releases, and met with other researchers to discuss their perspectives on my own research. I also spent significant amounts of time in 'out-of-the-way' spaces where people loitered, drank alcohol, and used drugs, which was especially productive for this research. Naga society is, broadly speaking, very relational. Communities are often closely linked, and people tend to know each other either directly or indirectly through family and friends. Gossip and prying, and avoiding gossip and prying, are significant parts of many Nagas' social lives, especially younger Nagas. This means that people often must be discrete when socializing informally or with people they might not want to be seen with, when drinking alcohol, when experimenting with drugs (often over-the-counter pharmaceuticals such as Spasmoproxyvon, a commonly abused anti-spasmodic, and 'Kodex' cough syrup), when smoking cigarettes, and when otherwise loitering and passing time. Hence, abandoned construction sites, disused infrastructure, and overgrown parks were excellent sites to meet people and build trust.

These are sites that people gather in to get away from prying family and gossipy neighbours. Spending time in these sites offered opportunities to meet with, observe, and talk to people about gender, their families and the expectations their families placed on them, and their hopes for the future. Overall, my ethnography involved immersing myself in as many aspects of life in Nagaland as possible. Because of this immersive approach, I was presented with myriad chance and serendipitous experiences that shaped the research, and in this time and through such encounters, I witnessed changes in Nagaland that may have otherwise been missed.

The majority of data was collected and recorded in the city of Dimapur. Dimapur proved to be an ideal site for most of the research for this book for several reasons. First, Dimapur is the largest city in Nagaland. It is the only city in Nagaland that has a train station, and the only city in Nagaland that has a commercial airport. Nagaland's most reliable roads tend to connect to Dimapur, and Nagaland State Transport runs direct buses to Dimapur from most towns in the state, often six days a week. Hence, Dimapur is relatively accessible and is a place that many people from all over Nagaland often go to. Second, because of this connectivity, Dimapur offers a space in which to engage with a diverse population of Nagas from different tribes and different parts of Nagaland, some of whom are new settlers, others who have come to the city long ago, and others who have been settled in Dimapur for generations. Dimapur was initially a Kachari settlement, then yielded to the Ahom Kingdom in 1536 (Gait, 1906: 244). The remains of the Kachari settlement are still visible in parts of Dimapur today. In the late 19th century, Dimapur became a supply node for tours of British forces into the Naga Hills, where Jain and especially Marwari communities established themselves as powerful traders to British administration (Hunter, 1879: 96). People come to Dimapur from other parts of India and from other parts of Nagaland seeking work, better services and a more exciting place to live (Kikon and McDuie-Ra, 2021: 12) Because people from other towns often live together and settle closely when they come to the city, Dimapur's suburbs are divided, roughly, according to ethnic, tribe and clan affiliations. This diversity offered a rough cross-section of Nagaland's tribal and clan demographics. Diversity also offered discussants a degree of anonymity. Discussants were much more comfortable and open to talk, and several explicitly stated that they were more comfortable speaking to me in Dimapur, where few people could recognize them and where it was easy for them to blend into the city's population. Third, Dimapur is where a number of Nagaland's borderland anxieties are played out, especially those involving migration, where the border is, and who controls the border. These anxieties surround control and identity of the city and its surroundings and are reflected in periods of heightened tension and violence towards non-Nagas, especially Bengali and Bangladeshi migrants. The anxieties that are present in Nagaland are magnified in Dimapur. Dimapur is a focal point for disputes over where Nagaland's borders begin and end, who can cross those borders and who enforces border politics. Hence, Dimapur was a site where the politics of migration, tribe and clan overlapped. Other research took place in Kohima and in the towns Phek and Kutsupo. Kohima is the capital of Nagaland and is home to a large population of government workers. It is the second largest city in the state and as well as being the political centre of the state, acts as a thoroughfare for people moving between Nagaland's more developed western districts and less connected eastern towns and villages. Phek is a town roughly a six-hour drive east of Kohima. It has a mostly agricultural economy and is surrounded by smaller villages that also depend on agriculture as their major economic activity. Kutsupo is one of these villages, about a day's walk west of Phek. In Phek and Kutsupo I made valuable connections with young men, members of village development organizations and customary leaders in 2012, which I revisited in 2016 and 2019.

Most interviews and discussions did not take place at a fixed location, except in a few cases in people's private homes. Interviews and discussions usually took place sporadically, after meeting and while getting to know the discussant. This happened in chai (tea) shops, at roadside eateries, and at sites where people congregated to pass time and socialize. Most often, discussions took place when walking in familiar neighbourhoods or in out-of-the-way places where participants felt comfortable being seen talking to a foreign researcher and where there was opportunity to move or leave surreptitiously if the need arose. Walking while discussing proved to be an invaluable research approach. Discussants were much more amenable to discussions when walking, especially if that meant that they could run errands at the same time or if discussions could take place when moving between work sites or going to local events. Walking handed much control of the discussion to my walking partners, who became walking guides during discussions, and often led the way to significant sites where other people gathered or led detours to sites to illustrate points they were trying to make. When walking, discussions flowed freely around the issues of men, political issues in the state, migration, corruption, and other items of concern, often prompted by objects passed while walking, or scenes and sites walked through. Visual cues and items elicited responses and discussions that were often revealing, insightful, and important. For example, while walking with a companion in Kohima, we encountered a small piece of graffiti reading 'nigger paan shop', which opened discussion of governance, migration and gender. My companion initially commented on the state of the building and street the graffiti appeared on and the role of the state in maintaining and repairing it; then on migration, my companion thought the topic of the graffiti was probably illegal Bangladeshi immigrants (IBIs); finally on gender and society, as we passed the graffiti, my companion discussed the risks he perceived Bangladeshi migrants presented to Naga women and the wider Naga community and the role of Naga men in fighting the 'IBI menace', both to protect the Naga women he saw as at risk of attack by IBIs, and to preserve the Naga society he saw as under siege by IBIs. While the graffiti itself was largely ambiguous, and it was just as likely that the graffiti was written on the door by children or teenagers with little meaning or political intention, the response that the graffiti elicited, seen and discussed while walking, brought to the surface insights and opinions that may otherwise have gone undiscussed. Walking alone and the responses it elicited also offered valuable insights. Walking alone near Dimapur train station at night drew attention and concern from friends and associates. 'You can't walk alone there at night, it's a dangerous place' was a typical response by friends to my accounts of walking near the station or in the central parts of Dimapur after dark. Other commentators replied, 'he can walk there, but women shouldn't ... it's a dangerous place for women at night'. Thus, the act of walking alone itself and the responses to walking at night highlighted the rules that govern spaces, the politics of access, gendered experiences, and the constantly shifting role of the immersed researcher themselves between observer, subject, and object of discussion. By walking, all of these issues were raised.

Being foreign, white and a male in Nagaland had an impact on the research. My positionality, as an obvious foreigner, as an educated researcher, and as male, served to both open-up some research possibilities and to close others off. On the one hand, participants were often eager to 'bring along' the foreign researcher on errands, to events, and to meetings. My foreign status, white skin, and Western education lent 'weight' in meetings with local bureaucrats, state officials, and businesspeople. This allowed access to numerous sites that would have been otherwise inaccessible. People were also often eager to talk to a foreigner and have their voices heard by somebody from outside of their community. After some time, many people were eager to share their own opinions about gender and change in Nagaland, in ways that I doubt they would have shared as openly if I were an 'insider' from their own tribe or clan, or a Naga, or a woman, or any variation of those three. Essentially, being an 'outsider' brought with it a naïve impartiality that allowed people to share things they would otherwise be less willing to share. On the other hand, my position as an outsider, as obviously not Naga, was also initially met with suspicion. Meetings with groups of men were often interrupted by exchanges in Nagamese or village languages, which were either too quick for my own rudimentary understanding, or completely unknown to me. Sometimes these language-swaps were accompanied by rough and short translations that obviously omitted many details, or dismissive statements such as 'they're talking about something else, it's not important'. Being an outsider also presented the risk that conversations and responses to questions may also have been shaped by motives to please me as a foreign researcher, to provide the researcher with perspectives or insights that discussants felt were what I might be looking for, or to confirm what participants may have perceived to be a hypothesis. Middleton and Pradhan (2014) refer to the tendency of hosts, subjects, and research assistants to accede to the assumed motives of the researcher as 'delivering *mumbo-jumbo*', in other words, playing along with assumptions that researchers come to investigate the most stereotypical, loudest, and most 'exotic' parts of a culture. This *mumbo jumbo* was encountered on several occasions, with many respondents providing unprompted and extended retellings of Nagaland's nationalist struggle and colourful histories of headhunting tribals. Responses may also have been exaggerated to understate issues that might be considered negative, embarrassing, or offensive. Finally, working in a space where armed conflict occasionally occurs, and occasionally interviewing current and former insurgents, there was a risk that responses would be affected by perceptions of risk and fears of retribution for speaking critically about police, insurgents, politicians, or fears of being perceived as doing so. While all ethnographic work poses some risk of reliability as responses are tied to personal experiences, this was controlled as much as it could be by follow up interviews, by discussing similar issues with as many participants as possible, by consulting non-verbal sources such as media reports, local writing, and observing local political posters, witnessing political rallies, local graffiti, and discussing the research with local academics, students, and journalists.

Outline

This book constitutes six chapters divided into two parts. Part 1, 'Periphery', constituting chapters 1, 2 and 3, discusses the construction of the Naga Hills, later Nagaland, as a remote 'frontier' space through colonial border-making policies and post-colonial exceptional laws through Chapters 1 and 2. Part 1 focuses on the ways the Naga hills were imagined and reframed through various colonial cartographic projects, and where and how these projects continue to hold weight today. Chapter 2, 'Becoming a Borderland', discusses the colonial frontier-making project in the Naga Hills, where an 'Inner Line' was created to divide the Naga Hills from the plains of Assam, and later post-Independence continuations of these policies, cartographies, and emergency laws. Essentially, where colonial efforts produced a sense of remoteness as being 'cut-off' from the plains surrounding Nagaland, post-colonial efforts produced a sense of remoteness as being outside of and cut-off from legal protections and rights. Chapter 3, 'Legacies of Conflict', discusses the complex legacies of decades of nationalist conflict that continue in Nagaland, including multiple sovereign contestants, disagreements over Nagaland's borders with neighbouring states, and the pervasive presence of an alternative map for a Naga homeland, 'Nagalim', that challenges India's cartographic limits. In this complex scenario, a highly masculinized political culture has emerged, one that encourages 'strongman' politics and an especially salient gendered social order. Part 2, 'Proximity', constituting Chapters 4, 5, and 6, discusses new gender dynamics emerging in Nagaland as the state undergoes complex and contested post-conflict changes. Gender in Nagaland is especially sensitive, as a cohesive but contested 'Naga' identity takes form alongside challenges to patriarchal customary institutions, exceptional laws and militarization, in- and out-migration, and the ongoing legacies of decades of conflict. Chapter 4, 'Nagaland Opening Up', discusses the complex connections and networks in Nagaland that have emerged and changed since ceasefire, including accelerating economic ties to India alongside efforts to define and protect a distinct Naga identity. The state's opening up, in various forms, has encouraged new conflicts and contestations, over jobs and resources, representation, and over fears of demographic changes in Nagaland. Gender and men's traditional and often self-assumed roles as guardians of Naga territory, culture, and society are central in these conflicts and contestations. Chapter 5 discusses the complex gendered contestations occurring within the Naga community as the state opens up to new political ideals, new cultural norms, and new challenges to long-held patriarchal gender norms. The chapter also explores the ways agitations for equal representation contend with a rigidly gendered social order that, as Nagaland's various borders soften and become more porous, is seen by many as a distinct cornerstone of Naga identity. Chapter 6 discusses the ways migration into Nagaland from other parts of India and from Bangladesh have created an explosive political narrative of 'outsiders' and threats to Nagaland's demographic balance. This

narrative is led by highly gendered notions of Naga men as protectors of
Naga territory, culture, and society from outside intruders. I conclude this
book with a reflection on the ways Nagaland exemplifies the making and
unmaking of borders – cartographic, legal, and cultural – and the ways this
ongoing process creates new forms of liberation and marginalization that
inform critical approaches to gender, place, and identity.

References

Agamben, G. (2005). *State of exception*. London: University of Chicago Press.

Agrawal, A. and Kumar, V. (2017). 'Cartographic conflicts within a union: Finding land for Nagaland in India'. *Political Geography* 61: 123–147. DOI: 10.1016/j.
polgeo.2017.06.015.

Angelova, I. (2015). 'Building a "home" away from home: The experiences of young
Naga migrants in Delhi'. *Journal of the Anthropological Society of Oxford* 7(2):
153–167.

Appadurai, A. (2006). *Fear of small numbers: An essay on the geography of Anger*.
Duke University Press. Available at: http://ebookcentral.proquest.com/lib/unsw/
detail.action?docID=1168400.

Baruah, S. (2007). *Durable disorder: Understanding the politics of Northeast India*. New
Delhi: Oxford University Press. DOI: 10.1093/acprof:oso/9780195690828.001.0001.

Belcher, O. Martin, L. and Tazzioli, M. (2015). 'Editorial: Border struggles:
Epistemologies, ontologies, and politics'. Available at: https://web.archive.
org/web/20151009221120/http://www.darkmatter101.org/site/2015/10/05/
editorial-border-struggles-epistemologies-ontologies-and-politics/ (accessed
11 December 2022).

Bijukumar, V. (2019). 'Intrigues of indigeneity and patriarchy in Khasi society'.
Economic & Political Weekly 54(10): 10–13.

Brown, S. (2013). 'Treading a fine line: State-making and conflict within eastern
Burma'. In: Korf, B. and Raeymaekers, T. (eds) *Violence on the margins: States,
conflict, and borderlands*, 87–117.

Chalfin, B. (2010). *Neoliberal frontiers: An ethnography of sovereignty in West Africa*.
Chicago: University of Chicago Press.

Chasie, C. and Hazarika, S. (2009). *The state strikes back: India and the Naga
insurgency*. Washington D.C.: East-West Center.

Dunn, E.C. and Cons, J. (2014). 'Aleatory sovereignty and the rule of sensitive spaces'.
Antipode 46(1): 92–109. DOI: 10.1111/anti.12028.

Eilenberg, M. (2014). 'Frontier constellations: agrarian expansion and sovereignty on
the Indonesian-Malaysian border'. *The Journal of Peasant Studies* 41(2): 157–182.

Faludi, S. (1991). *Backlash: The undeclared war against American women*. New York: Three Rivers Press. DOI: 10.1177/036168439201600304.

Fuller, C.J. (2016). 'History, anthropology, colonialism, and the study of India'. *History and Theory* 55(3): 452–464. DOI: 10.1111/hith.10821.

Gearoid, M. (2018). 'Ethnographic peace research: The underappreciated benefits of long-term Fieldwork'. *International Peacekeeping* 25(5): 653–676.

Gill, P. (2005). 'Women in the time of conflict: The case of Nagaland'. *India International Centre Quarterly* 323(2): 213–226.

Government of India (1958). The Armed Forces (Assam and Manipur) Special Powers Act, 1958. 28.

Government of India (2019). 'About BRO'. Available at: www.bro.gov.in/index2. asp?lang=1&sublinkid=5&slid=895&projectid=9%0D (accessed 7 July 2020).

Government of Nagaland (2016). 'Chapter 10: Indigenous inhabitant matters'. Available at: https://dpar.nagaland.gov.in/chapter-10-indigenous-inhabitant-matters/ (accessed 23 May 2020).

Hammersley, M. (2018). 'What is ethnography? Can it survive? Should it?' *Ethnography and Education* 13(1). Taylor & Francis: 1–17. DOI: 10.1080/17457823.2017.1298458.

Hammersley, M. and Atkinson, P. (2007). *Ethnography: Principles in practice*. 3rd ed. New York: Routledge. DOI: 10.2307/2070079.

Hogan, M.P. and Pursell, T. (2008). 'The "real Alaskan" in the "last frontier"'. *Men and Masculinities* 11(1): 63–85.

Hokowhitu, B. (2012). 'Producing elite indigenous masculinities'. *Settler Colonial Studies* 2(2): 23–48. DOI: 10.1080/2201473X.2012.10648840.

Human Rights Watch (2008). 'India: Getting away with murder, 50 years of the Armed Forces Special Powers Act', August 2008, available at: https://www.refworld.org/docid/48a93a402.html (accessed 19 January 2023).

Hunter, W.W. (1879). *A statistical account of Assam in two volumes (I)*. London: Trubner & Co.

Ingold, T. (2014). 'That's enough about ethnography!' *Hau: Journal of Ethnographic Theory* 4(1): 383–395. DOI: 10.14318/hau4.1.021.

Iralu, K. (2017). *Effects of the Armed Forces Special Powers Act on gender: Influence of social ecology on psychological well-being of women in Nagaland*. University of Tromso: Centre for Peace Studies.

Jones, R. (2012). 'Spaces of refusal: Rethinking sovereign power and resistance at the border'. *Annals of the Association of American Geographers* 102(3): 685–699. DOI: 10.1080/00045608.2011.600193.

Jonsson, H. (2014). *Slow anthropology: Negotiating difference with the Iu Mien*. Cornell: Cornell University Press. DOI: 10.1355/sj30-3j.

Kikon, D. (2015). *Life and dignity: Women's testimonies of sexual violence in Dimapur (Nagaland)*. Guwahati: North Eastern Social Research Centre.

Kikon, D. (2019). *Living with oil and coal: Resource politics and militarization in Northeast India.* Seattle: University of Washington Press.

Kikon, D. and McDuie-Ra, D. (2021). *Ceasefire city: Militarism, capitalism, and urbanism in Dimapur.* New Delhi: Oxford University Press.

Longkumer, A. (2013). 'Who sings for the Hornbill?: The performance and politics of culture in Nagaland, Northeast India – Part I'. The South Asianist Blog. Available at: https://thesouthasianist.wordpress.com/2013/02/14/who-sings-for-the-hornbill-the-performance-and-politics-of-culture-in-nagaland-northeast-india-part-i/.

Longkumer, A. (2018). '"Along Kingdom's Highway": The proliferation of Christianity, education, and print amongst the Nagas in Northeast India'. *Contemporary South Asia* 27(2): 160–178. DOI: 10.1080/09584935.2018.1471041.

Manchanda, R. (2004). 'We do more because we can: Naga women in the peace process'. In: *South Asian Forum for Human Rights*, Kathmandu, 2004.

Manchanda, R. (2005). *Naga women making a difference: Peace building in Northeast India* (ed. S.N. Anderlini). Greensboro, North Carolina: Women Waging Peace Policy Commission.

Mathur, N. (2010). 'Shopping malls, credit cards and global brands: Consumer culture and lifestyle of India's new middle class'. *South Asia Research* 30(3): 211–231. DOI: 10.1177/026272801003000301.

Mauss, M. (1926). *Manuel d'ethnographie.* Paris: Editions Sociales.

McDuie-Ra, D. (2012c). 'Violence against women in the militarized Indian frontier: Beyond "Indian culture" in the experiences of ethnic minority women'. *Violence Against Women* 18(3): 322–345. DOI: 10.1177/1077801212443114.

McDuie-Ra, D. (2016b). Border*land city in new India: Frontier to gateway.* Amsterdam: Amsterdam University Press.

Middleton, T. (2013a). 'Anxious belongings: Anxiety and the politics of belonging in subnationalist Darjeeling'. *American Anthropologist* 115(4): 608–621. DOI: 10.1111/aman.12051.

Middleton, T. (2013b). 'States of difference: Refiguring ethnicity and its "crisis" at India's borders'. *Political Geography* 35: 14–24. DOI: 10.1016/j.polgeo.2013.01.001.

Middleton, T. and Pradhan, E. (2014) 'Dynamic duos: On partnership and the possibilities of postcolonial ethnography'. *Ethnography* 15(3): 355–374. DOI: 10.1177/1466138114533451.

Myrttinen, H. (2012). 'Violence, masculinities and general patriarchy in post-conflict Timor-Leste'. In: Ford, M. and Lyons, L. (eds) *Men and Masculinities in Southeast Asia.* London: Routledge.

Nayak, M. and Suchland, J. (2006). 'Gender violence and hegemonic projects'. *International Feminist Journal of Politics* 8(4): 467–485. DOI: 10.1080/14616740600945024.

North East Network (2016). 'Enquiry into the Status of Women in Nagaland: An exploratory study of women in 3 districts of rural Nagaland done in 6 villages during January 2014 to March 2016'. Guwahati.

Palmer, N. (2014). 'Re-examining resistance in post-genocide Rwanda'. *Journal of Eastern African Studies* 8(2): 231–245. DOI: 10.1080/17531055.2014.891716.

Parliament of India (2022). *Two hundred thirty seventh report on police – Training, modernisation and reforms. February.* New Delhi. Available at: https://rajyasabha. nic.in/rsnew/Committee_site/Committee_File/ReportFile/15/161/237_2022_2_17. pdf (accessed 25 April 2022).

Philip, S. (2018). 'Caught in-between: social developments and young men in urban India'. *Journal of Gender Studies* 27(3): 362–370. DOI: 10.1080/09589236.2017.1391689.

Phillips, K. (2004). 'The India-Naga conflict: A long- standing war with few prospects of imminent solution'. CHRI News. Available at: http://www.humanright-sinitiative.org/old/publications/nl/articles/india/summer2004.pdf (accessed 14 July 2019).

Plonski, S. and Yousuf, Z. (2017). *Bringing in the margins: Peacebuilding and transition in borderlands.* London: Accord.

Rasmussen, M.B. and Lund, C. (2018). 'Reconfiguring frontier spaces: The territorialization of resource control'. *World Development* 101: 388–399. DOI: 10.1016/j. worlddev.2017.01.018.

Roll, K. and Swenson, G. (2019). 'Fieldwork after conflict: Contextualising the challenges of access and data quality'. *Disasters* 43(2): 240–260. DOI: 10.1111/ disa.12321.

Rosaldo, R. (1989). *Culture and truth: The remaking of social analysis.* Boston: Beacon Press.

Sarmah, B. (2016). 'The cauldron of conflict: Politics of peace, governance and development in India's North-East'. *Social Scientist* 4(11): 15–36.

Schatz, E. (2009). *Political ethnography: What immersion contributes to the study of power.* Los Angeles: University of California Press.

Shimray, U.A. (2007). *Naga population and integration movement.* New Delhi: Mittal Publications.

Tohring, S.R. (2010). *Violence and identity in North-East India: Naga-Kuki conflict.* New Delhi: Mittal Publications

Tsing, A.L. (1993). *In the realm of the Diamond Queen: Marginality in an out-of-the-way place.* Princeton: Princeton University Press.

van Houtum, H. and van Naerssen, T. (2002). 'Bordering, ordering and othering'. *Tijdschrift voor Economische en Sociale Geografie* 93(2): 125–136.

van Schendel, W. and Abraham, I. (2005). *Illicit flows and criminal things: States, borders, and the other side of globalization.* Bloomington: India University Press.

Weiss, L. (2005). 'The state-augmenting effects of globalisation'. *New Political Economy* 10(3): 345–353. DOI: 10.1080/13563460500204233.

Whitehead, T.L. (2004). 'What is ethnography? Methodological, ontological and epistemological attributes'. *Cultural Ecology of Health and Change*: 1–29.

Whitehead, T.L. (2005). 'Basic classical ethnographic research methods: Secondary data analysis, fieldwork, observation/participant observation, and informal and semi-structured interviewing'. Cultural Ecology of Health and Change: Ethnographically Informed Community and Cultural Assessment Research Systems (EICCARS) working paper series. Available at: http://www.cusag.umd.edu/documents/workingpapers/classicalethnomethods.pdf.

Wilkinson, M. (2015) 'Negotiating with the Other: Centre-periphery perceptions, peacemaking policies and pervasive conflict in the Chittagong Hill Tracts, Bangladesh'. *International Review of Social Research Special Issue – Non State Armed Groups in National and International Politics* 5(2): 179–190.

Wouters, J.J.P. (2018) *In the shadows of Naga insurgency: Tribes, state, and violence in Northeast India*. New Delhi: Oxford University Press.

Wouters, J.J.P. and Subba, T.B. (2013) 'The "Indian face," India's Northeast, and "The Idea of India"'. *Asian Anthropology* 12(2): 126–140. DOI: 10.1080/1683478X.2013.849484.

Wouters, J.J.P. (2022) 'How to interpret a lynching?' In: *Flows and frictions in Trans-Himalayan spaces: Histories of networking and border crossing*. Amsterdam University Press, 167–202. DOI: 10.5117/9789463724371_ch07.

Yimchunger, J. (2020) 'Naga youth engagement with Korean popular culture: An alternative avenue'. *International Journal of Media and Cultural Politics* 16(2): 233–251. DOI: 10.1386/macp_00026_1.

Zabiliute, E. (2016) 'Wandering in a mall: aspirations and family among young urban poor men in Delhi'. *Contemporary South Asia* 24(3): 271–284. DOI: 10.1080/09584935.2016.1208638.

2   Becoming a Borderland

Abstract

Chapter 2, 'Becoming a Borderland', discusses the colonial frontier-making project in the Naga Hills, where an 'Inner Line' was created to divide the Naga Hills from the plains of Assam, and later post-Independence continuations of these policies, cartographies, and emergency laws. Essentially, where colonial efforts produced a sense of remoteness as being 'cut-off' from the plains surrounding Nagaland, post-colonial efforts produced a sense of remoteness as being outside of and cut-off from legal protections and rights.

Keywords: Zomia, highlands, colonization, exception.

'ILP Identifies illegal immigrants'

Between November and December 2019, Assam was in the midst of one of its most violent periods in recent history as students rallied against the Bharatiya Janata Party (BJP) Government's Citizenship Amendment Bill (CAB).[1] The BJP claimed the Bill intended to grant Indian citizenship to persecuted religious minorities including Hindus, Jains, Sikhs, and Christians who came to India from Pakistan, Afghanistan, and Bangladesh before 2015 (*Times of India*, 2020). Critics argued that the Bill was skewed towards allowing Hindus in particular to achieve citizenship in an attempt to import Hindu voters into India and would open the doors to droves of migrants from Bangladesh coming into Assam and its neighbouring states (*Times of India*, 2019). Aggravating the CAB situation was the ongoing update of the National Register of Citizens (NRC) in Assam, an official record of legal citizens of India, the first time the Register had been updated since 1955. Critics of the NRC noted that Muslim names had been deliberately left off

---

1   Now the Citizenship Amendment Act (CAA) after being passed in India's federal upper house, the Rajya Sabha, on 11 December 2019.

Wilkinson, Matthew: *Borderland Anxieties. Shifting Understandings of Gender, Place and Identity at the India-Burma Border.* Amsterdam: Amsterdam University Press, 2023
DOI: 10.5117/9789463729789_CH02

the list of citizens, and argued that the Register was an attempt to deny citizenship to Indian Muslims who had lived in Assam for generations (Changoiwala, 2020). Taken together, the CAB appeared to be an attempt to import Hindu voters, while the NRC simultaneously stripped Muslims and people with Muslim names of their citizenship. The CAB and NRC were pivotal triggers in a state and a region that has had a tense relationship with the Indian centre for decades, especially regarding migration politics (Mahanta, 2013). Protestors in Assam's capital, Guwahati, blocked GS road, the largest road in the city, and burned effigies of Prime Minister Modi in the surrounding streets and suburbs. Truckloads of Indian soldiers were brought into the city and curfews were announced to quell the violence, shutting shopfronts, closing transportation, and relegating people to their homes for eleven days. In other parts of the state, roads and bridges were blocked and vandalized and several train stations were set alight. In neighbouring states, student unions – some of the largest and most active grassroots political organizations in Northeast India – held rallies and sitting protests in solidarity with the anti-CAB movement. Following the protests and curfew, Assam woke to sweep up the damage of nearly two weeks of protest. The freshly painted Guwahati, preparations made in advance of Japanese Prime Minister Shinzo-Abe's visit that was cancelled due to the violence, was covered in anti-CAB graffiti and cartoon images of Indian Prime Minister Modi featuring a Hitler-esque moustache.

For tribal communities in Assam and in Assam's surrounding states – Meghalaya, Tripura, Mizoram, Manipur, Nagaland and Arunachal Pradesh, who already felt vulnerable to being 'crowded out' by migrant populations coming from the plains, the CAB magnified existing anxieties surrounding migration and representation. Several tribal communities demanded their respective governments decry the CAB and uphold and expand protections from a perceived oncoming wave of post-CAB migrants. Central to these protections was the Inner Line Permit (ILP) system, formally the Bengal Eastern Frontiers Regulations Act (1873), a colonial-era policy aimed at preventing movement between lowland plains and highland tribal territories. Non-local residents, including Indian citizens, are required to obtain an Inner line Permit, colloquially an 'ILP', before entering an ILP area. At town centres and gathering points across Assam's state borders, rallies were held demanding the ILP system be expanded to prevent post-CAB migrants pouring into the state from Assam. Demands to expand the ILP system were not new. In many of these areas, the CAB protests in Assam reignited calls for the reinstatement and expansion of the ILP that were decades old. Noticeboards and walls at transport hubs throughout Northeast India were plastered with posters and petitions denouncing illegal migrants and promoting the ILP as a way of preventing or exposing illegal migrants. In Assam, several tribal and student organizations petitioned the Supreme Court to reinstate the ILP in the districts of Kamrup, Darrang, Nagaon, Sibsagar, Lakhimpur and Cachar. After years of discussion and debate in the neighbouring state of Meghalaya, the Meghalaya Assembly passed a motion to urge the Government of India to implement the ILP system in its borders. In the neighbouring state of Manipur, following decades of violent demands for the ILP to be extended from the state's tribal areas to cover the entire state, the ILP was reinstated throughout Manipur effective from 1 January 2020. In Nagaland, also following years of demands by tribal groups, the ILP was hastily extended to include Dimapur district and its application extended from 'Indian nationals' to 'every non-indigenous person' effective from 9 December 2019. Non-indigenous people who lived in Nagaland were given recourse to stay without an ILP if they could show they had lived in the state prior to 21 November 1979, forty years prior to the Bill to extend the ILP.

Demands to expand the ILP system in the wake of the CAB debate were a smaller part of the ongoing bordering project in Northeast India, where state borders are closed off and opened up as central governments, state governments, and local communities vie for control and legitimacy. This project encompasses geography, identity, and state-making priorities. Frontier and borderland areas are represented as outside and peripheral to the state centre, as 'untamed', lawless, and as wanting of the state's presence and order. This project has ebbed and flowed since before India's independence, with permit systems, designated areas such as 'Backward Tracts' and 'Scheduled Districts', and frontier areas being drawn, reinterpreted, and erased according to the needs of various administrations. In this chapter, I discuss this bordering project in Nagaland and in the wider Northeast. I first discuss the role of geography in creating a natural frontier and borderland, a highland region that acts as a stopping point for precolonial states and a dividing line between South and Southeast Asia. I then discuss the role of colonial cartography and anthropology in mapping this natural borderland and enforcing stringent checks on movement, including the Inner Line Permit system, that further contributed to political, cultural, and social divides between highland areas of Northeast India and the plains below. This bordering process allowed an ad hoc approach to governing the Naga Hills District, the maintenance of customary political institutions, and encouraged Christianity in Naga communities. Finally, I discuss the post-Independence bordering project and the ways that responses to real and perceived state evasion and resistance at the borderland contribute to exceptional treatment and reinforce existing divides between the centre and periphery in Northeast India.

Hills

The highlands along the India/Burma border are marked by jagged and steep hills, dense forests, and deep valleys. This mountainous terrain is a result of the ongoing collision between the Indian continental plate and the Asian Sunda plate (Najman et al., 2020). As the plates collide, the subduction of the Indian plate beneath the Sunda plate pushes the ground up, creating the Indo-Burman ranges. The ranges extend from the south-western tip of Burma at present day Parthein to the south-eastern tip of the Himalayas at Arunachal Pradesh, where they form a rough natural boundary between India and China. At their southern point the ranges cascade into the Chittagong coastal plain and the Bay of Bengal. On their north-western boundary, the ranges descend into the Assam Valley, divided lengthways by the Brahmaputra river. To the east, the ranges subside into the Central Myanmar Basin and the Irrawaddy River system. The ranges are a part of the larger Southeast Asian massif, a loosely bound collection of mountain ranges, high plateaus and valleys extending from the highlands of Cambodia and Vietnam in Southeast Asia to the Tianshian mountain range in Central Asia. Willem van Schendel has termed this area 'Zomia' (2002b), a roughly mapped 'non-state' space marked by its difficult geography – mountainous, with forbidding cliffs and steep inclines that act as a geographic boundary between South and Southeast Asia. Nagaland constitutes part of this highland region, seated along the eastern border of India and the western border of Burma. Nagaland's present day borders, though contested by groups within Nagaland and also by Nagaland's neighbouring states, loosely include the foothills of the Patkai mountain ranges to the west, a porous mountainous border with Myanmar to the east, the Pahain mountains of Arunachal Pradesh to the north, and the Dimapur valley and Dzoku valley to the south.

In one of the earliest comprehensive studies of the Indo-Burman ranges, Brunnschweiler (1966: 138) describes 'jungle-clad slopes [that] present a formidable geographical and ethnological barrier. For that reason they have long been known as the divide between the Middle East and the Far East'. Brunnschweiler's description, while somewhat archaic in its language, is an apt reflection of the imposing and forbidding nature of the ranges. For centuries the ranges have acted as an effective stopping point for plains-based court centres and state structures, who have rarely had the resources and supply chains capable of maintaining a state-presence in the highlands. The communities in these highlands have, in various smaller and larger waves across centuries, migrated uphill seeking shelter from aggressive plains-state expansion, corvée labour, taxes, conscription, and diseases common to the surrounding lowlands (Scott, 2009: 8). Early colonial accounts of communities living in these highlands betray the politics of Zomia. Pemberton (1827) describes communities living on the Indo-Burman ranges as:

> [a] singular race of people ... extending from the north-western extremity of Kachar to the frontiers of Chittagong, from their poverty and peculiar situation, have escaped the sufferings inflicted by a powerful enemy on the more wealthy occupiers of the plains below them. With a sagacity which has at once insured them both health and security, they have in every instance established themselves upon the most inaccessible peaks of the mountainous belt they inhabit, and from these elevated positions can see and guard against approaching danger long before it is sufficiently near to be felt. Various attempts, in the days of their prosperity and power, were made by the Rajahs of Munipore [Manipur], Kachar [Cachar], and Tipperah [Tripura], to reduce these savages to a state of vassalage, but uniformly without success – they steadily refused to acknowledge allegiance to either power, and policy restrained the two first from using coercive measures, where success was, at least, doubtful, and failure would effectually have closed against them the only direct communications between their respective countries.
>
> (quoted in Elwin, 1969: 42)

These communities are often distinct from those in the surrounding plains in terms of languages, customs, histories, religions, modes of agriculture and diet, but among other highland groups have 'shared ideas, related lifeways, and long-standing cultural ties' (van Schendel, 2002a: 649). Livelihoods in these highlands are state-evasive, either by design or by lack of alternative. Some of these include the practice of shifting, slash-and-burn (jhum) forms of agriculture that are hard for states to tax and require regular move-ment for new tracts of arable land; they follow different religions, often Christianity, Buddhism or Animism rather than the 'great plains' religions of Hinduism and Islam; they speak different languages, sometimes distinct to single villages. In many parts of these highlands written languages were uncommon and oral histories were widely relied on before the arrival of

Christian and Buddhist missions in the 19th century (Scott, 2009: 220). Many highland tribal communities continue to rely on oral histories to pass on origins stories and epics (Teron, 2014). Knowledge-making about these sites, through colonial and postcolonial anthropologies, state-sponsored expeditions and studies, reproduces the state's border-making project. This is done by presenting these spaces as peripheral, in-between spaces, and also as geographically, culturally, and temporally distinct from the centre. Representations of the space as distinct from surrounding territories are used to justify efforts to induce fragmentation and to appropriate the space using various civil and military means, including controlling movement into and out of the space. Van Schendel (2002b: 650–651) describes this process as creating 'marshes, the borderlands that separate the region from other world regions'. By framing these sites as timeless, untouched, or otherwise forgotten – as 'repositories of civilizational antiquity' – these spaces are marked as distinct in terms of populations, histories, and states of development (Misra, 2011: 5). In doing so, a borderland space is brought into existence, marked by geography that is often state-forbidding, but also, made through exceptional laws and treatments enforced by the state, through discourses of centre-periphery, and through the internalization of this discourse by borderland communities.

Nagaland's precolonial and colonial history exemplifies this frontiering and bordering project. The communities that form the Naga tribes in Nagaland today are the outcome of waves of migration into the hills (Hutton, 1921: 5–9). As a result, the state is a melting pot of traditions, languages, modes of governance, and ideological and political projects (Elwin, 1969; von Fürer-Haimendorf, 1938). Origin stories of the settlement of the Naga Hills are contentious and differ between many tribes, although some common threads exist. Several tribes refer to Makhel, in the modern-day neighbouring state of Manipur, as their ultimate ancestral home (Wettstein, 2012). These stories are shared between the Poumai Naga in Manipur, and the Angami and Chakhesang tribes in Nagaland. Prior to the colonial era, the Naga Hills were largely inaccessible and beyond the reach of plains-based courts and kingdoms. The Ahom kingdom, based in the Assam valley, ended at the Naga foothills, where terrain became too steep and populations too sparse to allow further expansion. Some local interactions did take place, including *posa* tax, occasional raids and some trading relationships that brought salt, cotton, herbs, ivory, beeswax, mats, and daos from the Naga Hills into Assam, though these taxing, raiding and trading relationships were informal and often disrupted (Das, 2011). Beginning in 1817, three invasions of Assam by Burmese forces took place, ejecting the Ahom leadership from the Assam valley. Burmese aggression at Assam's borders with Bengal, Chittagong and Sylhet encouraged a stern response by British forces, resulting in the first Anglo-Burmese war between 1824 and 1826.[2] British forces pushed Burmese troops out of Assam and into Burma, ending the war with the signing of the Treaty of Yandabo on 24 February 1826 between the British East India Company and the Kingdom of Ava (Burma). The Treaty ceded control of Assam, Manipur, Rakhine (Arakan) and Taninthayi (Tenasserim) to the British East India Company (British East India Company, 1826). Assam was subsequently made a part of British Bengal under the Bengal Presidency.

On acquiring Assam, the British East India Company was presented with a vast topography stretching from the plains surrounding the lower Brahmaputra in the southwest to the highlands of present-day Arunachal Pradesh to the northeast. The southeast was bounded by the hill tracts of the unmapped Garo Hills, Khasi and Jaintia Hills, Cachar, and Naga Hills. In the northwest the districts Goalpara, Kamrup, and Darang formed a mountainous border with Tibet. Years of Ahom isolationism and Burmese occupation left much of the Assam valley between the mountain ranges to waste. The Ahom mint was defunct and Assam's economy was reduced to subsistence rice agriculture and a small yield of opium and mustard seed (Guha, 1967). What little infrastructure existed under Ahom leadership had been left in disrepair (Sharma, 2011: 2). Large parts of the province had been abandoned and many areas were effectively uninhabited (Gait, 1926: 222). In the first thorough survey of Assam following the signing of the Yandabo treaty, M'Cosh (1837: 13) describes the Company's new acquisition:

> This extensive valley, though some centuries ago richly cultivated by an industrious and enterprising people, is now throughout six-eighths or seven-eighths of its extent covered with a jungle of gigantic reeds, traversed only by the wild elephant or the buffalo; where a human footstep is unknown, and the atmosphere even to the natives themselves is pregnant with febrile miasmata and death. The ruins of splendid temples are discovered in wastes and forests long forgotten: large tanks overgrown and choked up with brushwood, point out the situations of once populous cities: and the furrows of the wild hog or the bear turn up the foundations of buildings unexpected and unknown.

2   This book does not delve into the Anglo-Burmese war in-depth; rather, it is discussed incidentally as an event that led to British annexation of Assam from 1826. A thorough and widely cited history of the Anglo-Burmese war is offered in Wilson, H. H., (1852) *Narrative of the Burmese War in 1824–26*, London, W. M. H. Allen & Co.

The Company endorsed a succession of expeditions to document Assam's potential wealth. Company expeditions found what the Company had suspected since its earliest interactions in Assam – that the territory was rich in forest resources and mineable wealth that had largely been untouched by the Ahom regime. However, Assam's lack of roads and the considerable expense incurred in reaching, extracting, and transporting these resources, left much of Assam out of reach to the Company. Assam's fortunes changed dramatically with the discovery of tea. In 1823 Scottish trader Robert Bruce learned that the Singpho tribe in North Assam cultivated and brewed tea much like the Chinese, who at that point held the monopoly over tea production (Bruce, 1840). Following confirmation of tea plants growing in Upper Assam, in 1834, a committee was appointed to enquire into the possibility of tea cultivation in India (Superintendent of the Assam Secretariat, 1896: 32). Successful experimentation of tea plantations took place in the districts Kamrup, Nagaon, Darang, Sibsagar, and Lakhimpur (Sarmah, 2016: 19). The Assam Tea Company was established in 1838 and the Wasteland Grant Rules (1838) were enacted to allow plantation investors to rent 'wasteland' from the Company at especially low rates. This 'wasteland' included communal forests, grazing land, jungle, and land used for jhum cultivation. As a result, tea plantations expanded dramatically throughout Upper Assam. Plantation acreage increased from 2,311 acres (1841) to 8,000 acres (1859) (Guha, 1985: 145–159). When the foothills were found to also be suitable for tea production, plantations were extended to the lower reaches of the Naga Hills, the foothills that divided the Assam plains from the highlands (Baruah, 2003: 325).

Communities in the Naga Hills, even before the colonial encounter, were perceived to be particularly resistant and difficult to manage. In 1837, two years prior to the first recorded encounters between British authorities and Nagas, McCosh writes that 'they [the Nagas] are the wildest and most barbarous of all the hill tribes, and looked upon with dread and horror by the neighbours of the plains, who consider them as ruthless robbers and murderers' (M'Cosh, 1837: 156). The Naga Hills were said to bring 'no profit and would be as costly as it is productive' for colonial state-makers (Dalhousie, 1851: 203). With the expansion of British tea plantations towards the Naga foothills, Naga raids on plantations and lowland communities ensued. Raids on British plantations, including kidnapping British officers and their family members, justified British incursions into the unmapped Naga Hills. Initially, British expeditions in the Naga Hills aimed to punish and prevent plantation raids. Summed up by Mackenzie (1884: 105), '[the government] had never contemplated anything more than the exercise of a general political control over the hill tribes, and, if necessary, the establishment of a military post to overcome the ill-disposed and give protection to the peaceable. Anything beyond this was not desired'. In 1866 the Naga Hills District was carved out of portions of North Cachar and the Angami Hills District. Possession of the Naga Hills was not the intention of the new district. The new district headquarters was sighted at Samagutung, present day Chümoukedima, with the goal of discouraging Naga raids on Assamese plantations while staying as little involved in the everyday matters of the Naga Hills as possible. Continued threats to plantations in Assam and speculations of headhunting, slave-raiding and warfare justified the expansion of colonial jurisdiction into the Naga Hills. Speculations of widespread headhunting and slave-raiding in the Naga Hills were maintained and perpetuated by colonial officers. Head-hunting and other violent acts did occur in the Naga Hills and the Northeastern Frontier, and there are confirmed instances of beheadings (Reed, 1942: 178). Colonial officers bore witness to human skulls on display in Morungs and dangling from trees at significant sites (ibid: 189). The true source of these heads, whether hunted by rivals, dug after a burial, or kept as a traditional memorial, are debatable (Thong, 2012; West, 1985, 1994; Zou, 2005). Reports of widespread and common head-hunting were seldom confirmed, and much of the discussion of head-hunting was informed by rumour, speculation, and a handful of earlier accounts written by colonial officers (Wilkinson, 2017a: 137). As a result, governance of the Naga Hills was ad hoc, almost entirely in the hands of commissioners on the ground, with few reporting responsibilities. In a telling example of this approach, the Naga Hills District's first commissioner Lieutenant Gregory was advised that his 'line of action may advantageously be left in great measure to his own good judgement' (Mackenzie, 1884: 120).

Inner Lines, Backward Tracts

To control movement between the Naga Hills and the plains Assam, the Bengal Eastern Frontier Regulations (1873) were applied to the western foothills of the Naga Hills, and also to the districts of Kamrup, Darrang, Nawgong (Nagaon), Sibsagar (Sivasagar), and Lakhimpur in Assam, and in the Khasi, Garo and Jaintia Hills in present day Meghalaya. The regulations enforced stringent controls over relations with frontier tribes, stopping rubber speculation and trading between colonial subjects and hills tribes, and restraining the spread of tea gardens outside of the reach of the Empire where taxing and protecting plantations was difficult. The Regulations constructed two lines of demarcation – an Inner Line, and an Outer Line. The Inner Line marked the limits of regular administration, where the state's reach largely ended. The Outer Line vaguely marked the ends of the British Empire entirely, although its borders were deliberately vague so as not to limit the possible future territories of the Empire or surrender potential territory to neighbouring states (Chakravarti, 1971). The Inner Line was shifted several times as communities were brought into the Empire and plantation land and lucrative resources were identified and secured, and confusion as to where the actual Line stood was common among officials – whether it coincided with the boundaries of revenue surveys, or the limits of regular cultivation, or the line of police outposts in the north of Assam (Kar, 2009b). The Naga Hill's eastern border was unmapped and its demarcations from Burma were much vaguer. The boundary between Assam and Burma was unsettled, though there was an acceptance that the border was geographically determined by the Naga Hills, Cachar Hills, and Manipur (Das, 2014: 64). Beyond the eastern border was un-administered territory (Mills, 1935: 419). Despite the British annexation of Burma in 1885, and Burma being brought into British India as a Lieutenant Governorship in 1897, the India/Burma border, especially along the Naga Hills, remained unmapped well into the 20th century. Only in 1935 did the Government of Burma Act firmly separate British India from Burma. Even following this separation, the Naga Hills' border with Burma were a matter of debate. The present-day border was officially mapped in 1958 by aerial survey and recognized by India and Burma officially in the 1967 Burma-India Boundary Agreement.

The Inner Line marked a temporal and civilizational divide, where ad hoc modes of governance allowed and encouraged the maintenance of local forms of order and customary institutions due to the difficulties encountered trying to administer the space. Communities beyond the line were seen as 'not yet suited for the elaborate legal rules laid down in the procedure codes ... they had to be governed in a simpler and more personal manner than those of the more civilized and longer-settled districts' (Gait, 1926: 333). Governance of these communities was ad hoc, with as little involvement by colonial authorities as was required to prevent movement between the hills and plains. As described by Alexander Mackenzie, Secretary of the Home Department of the Government of India (1884: 89–90):

> Beyond the line the tribes are left to manage their own affairs with only such interference on the part of the frontier officers on their political capacity as may be considered advisable with the view of establishing a

personal influence for good among the chiefs and tribes. Any attempt to
bring the country between the settled districts of British India and Burma
under our direct administration, even in the loosest way ... or to govern
it as British territory is to be steadily resisted. No European planter is to
be allowed to accept any grant beyond the line or under a tenure derived
from any chief or tribe.

With the Naga Hills largely cut off from the plains and the rest of India,
and with the special powers granted to colonial administrators, further
incursions were made possible. Various state technologies were employed
to govern the Naga Hills with few resources and with the goal of staying
uninvolved in local tribal politics. From 1874 the Naga Hills fell under
the purview of the Scheduled Districts Act (Government of India, 1874).
The Act conferred sweeping authority to local governors to enforce laws
and regulate as they saw fit in parts of British India that were hard to
govern, including the Inner Line territories, empowering local governors
to appoint and regulate officers, determine boundaries between Scheduled
Districts and run administration separately to regular administration in
the rest of India. Scheduled District status was applied to areas that 'had
never been brought within, or had from time to time been removed from,
the operation of the general Acts and Regulations and the jurisdiction of
the ordinary courts of Judicature' (Government of India, 1874).[3] In light
of the Act, various structures in the Naga Hills were altered and colonial
forms of governance were brought in. Colonial administrators introduced
new political structures to the Naga Hills. The offices of *Gaonbura*, or
village headman, and *Dobashi*, Assamese speaking intermediaries, were
introduced, forming a bridge between village politics and colonial administration. Through these policies, colonial administrators formalized the
isolation the Naga Hills from the outside and began a mode of governance
that merged colonial state structures with local customary institutions.
While the Naga Hills were difficult to access and isolated before colonial
administration, colonial policies actively cut the Naga Hills off from almost
any outside access. In light of animist religions, and real and perceived
instances of headhunting and slave raiding, colonial administrators allowed
and encouraged Christian missionaries to establish churches and schools
and convert Nagas to Christianity. Efforts to convert Naga communities

---

3   Later on, this legislation became the Government of India Act of 1919, which empowered
the Governor General in Council to declare any territory to be a 'Backward Tract' where 'laws
passed by the Indian legislature would not apply'.

to Christianity began early in the colonial administration of the Naga Hills. Captain Francis Jenkins, who led the first British expedition into the Naga Hills in 1832, sent correspondence to the board of the American Baptist Missions in 1835 requesting missionaries to convert Naga tribals. These early efforts were limited and unsuccessful though. The first mission established among Nagas in 1839 was abandoned two years later. Efforts were revived following a firmer colonial presence in the Naga Hills. In 1871, the American Baptist mission in Assam sent an Assamese evangelist to Ao Naga territory to convert and baptize Ao Nagas (Thong, 2010: 599). Welsh Presbyterian and American Baptist missionaries granted access to the Naga Hills from 1872 in efforts to convert Nagas to Christianity and provide a counterpoise to Hindu and Muslim groups in the plains (Longkumer 2018b). Following initial conversions, Naga pastors and missionaries led much of the conversion of tribal communities from animist faith systems to Christianity (Joshi, 2007). By the early 20th century, some conversions had taken place; however, resistance to Christianity was widespread (Longkumer, 2018a).

Essentially, the Naga Hills District was formed to cordon off a troubled zone, as cheaply and efficiently as possible, to protect tea plantations in Assam while being as little entangled in the complex tribal politics that abounded in the Naga Hills and other highland regions around Assam. These communities had resisted state incorporation before and were seen as having little prospect or value for incorporation into the colonial state in the near future. Colonial administration in the Naga Hills District set out to establish a loose control over the territory and prevent raids on the increasingly important resource hub that was the Brahmaputra valley. To achieve this, various state technologies were enacted. The Bengal Eastern Frontier Regulations (1873) drew an 'Inner Line' between the plains in Assam and the Naga foothills, across which movements were limited. The Scheduled Districts Act (1874) officially handed commissioners and governors free rein in the Naga Hills, creating a space where the laws that applied in the rest of India were re-interpreted and reconfigured according to the needs of local administrators, or simply did not apply at all. Finally, with few resources available, customary institutions and networks of village elites were brought closer into the fold of the state through the introduction of Gaonburas and Dobashis. The effect of these colonial technologies was the creation of a highland district that was distinct geographically and culturally, but also cartographically and legally, from the rest of India, where customary modes of governance were recognized and further empowered as adopted pieces of the colonial state.

Independence, Conflict

India's 1947 Independence brought with it expectations of dramatic political change for many communities in India. 'Backward Tracts', peripheries and other marginal areas including the Naga Hills District, that had been governed differently under British administration, held hopes for greater autonomy, various degrees of independence, and in some cases complete severance from the Indian Union. Naga nationalist actors made some of the earliest, loudest, and most sustained of these calls. As early as 1929, the Naga Club, formed in 1918 to bring together various Naga tribes as an umbrella independence movement, submitted a memorandum to the Simon Commission requesting the Naga Hills be given the option for self-determination after the British departure from India. In 1945, the Naga Hills District Tribal Council was formed at Wokha, changing its name to the Naga National Council (NNC) in 1946 and demanding complete autonomy from India. In June 1947 a negotiated settlement was attempted between the NNC and the Governor of Assam, Akbar Hydari, to set up an interim politico-administrative agreement in the form of the Naga-Hydari Accord. The Accord detailed nine points, covering (1) an independent judiciary, (2) executive roles, (3) legislative functions, (4) land rights, (5) taxation, (6) boundaries of the Naga Hills, (7) arms laws, (8) boundary terms upholding the Bengal Eastern Frontiers Regulations Act, and (9) a ten year period of the agreement after which 'the Naga Council [NNC] will be asked whether they require the above agreement to be extended for a further period or a new agreement regarding the future of Naga people arrived at' (Naga National Council, 1947).

Although the Accord handed significant control of administration to the NNC, the final point was contentious. Elements within the NNC pushed for the ninth point to allow the Naga Hills to secede altogether from the Indian Union. The Government of India interpreted the ninth point as an option to negotiate changes in administration, but not to secede altogether (Haokip, 2012: 310). This marked a critical juncture in Nagaland's independence push. The NNC, formerly a moderate actor in negotiations with the Government of India, began agitating for full independence without compromise under the leadership of Angami Zapu Phizo (Haokip, 2012: 310). Phizo declared Naga independence on 14 August 1947, one day before India officially declared its own independence from British rule. The Naga independence claim was rejected by the Government of India. In 1951 the NNC held a plebiscite to determine local support for independence, where 99 per cent of Nagas voted for separation from India (Joshi, 2013: 182). The following year, Naga communities boycotted the first Indian parliamentary election (Kikon, 2005: 2833).

In September 1953 an official declaration of independent sovereignty was made by the 'Khunak Kautang Ngeukhum'nt' (People's Sovereign Republic of Free Nagaland) being established by the NNC (Singh, 2004: 60). By 1956 Phizo had raised the Naga Federal Army and Naga Federal Government, acting as a state of its own in the Naga Hills. The rebellion in the Naga Hills, a former Backward Tract largely unnoticed and unknown to the rest of India threatened to inspire, and as it did later on, actively encourage other separatist rebellions in neighbouring states and in other parts of India (Kotwal, 2008).

In response to this resistance, the Government of India issued a number of exceptional laws and ordinances applicable to areas it deemed as 'disturbed'. First, the Government of India re-constituted the Armed Forces (Special Powers) Ordinance, originally developed in 1942 to suppress the Quit India movement. The Ordinance bestowed 'special powers' to Indian armed forces, including paramilitaries, to deal with state resistance. These special powers included the use of deadly force and provided complete immunity to officers – their acts could not be legally challenged, by anybody, except with the prior approval of the central government. In 1948, the Armed Forces Special Powers Act emerged from the Ordinance, then repealed in 1957, and resurrected a year later due to the deteriorating security situation in Assam from the Naga rebellion as the Armed Forces (Special Powers) Act (1958) (AFSPA). The Act grants the Indian Army extensive rights to search, detain, and to 'fire upon or otherwise use force even to causing of death' on suspicion of committing an offense or suspicion that one is 'about to commit' an offense (4I). Section 6 states that no prosecution, suit or other legal proceeding can be instituted without sanction of the Central Government (4(6)). In effect, the Act suspends any rights in the areas it is applied to, giving full impunity to the army, its officers, and 'any other officers of the Union [of India] so operating' (Government of India, 1958).

Second, the Sixth Schedule was introduced to the Indian Constitution in 1949 to grant scheduled tribal communities in Assam various degrees of autonomy and reservations in India's political system. Under the Sixth Schedule some groups, 'scheduled tribes', are allowed a degree of autonomy and self-government within an established framework of district and regional councils (Hausing, 2014). The Schedule, however, did not address a key demand of Naga nationalists – recognition of their self-determination claim at the end of a ten year period – and was rejected by the NNC (Hausing, 2014: 91). In response, on 26 July 1960, a Sixteen Point Agreement was signed between the Government of India and the Naga People's Convention, granting specific forms of autonomy, and statehood, to the Naga Hills. The first point of the Agreement forms the state of Nagaland out of the Naga Hills District and the Tuensang Area. The seventh point states that no act or law passed by the Indian Union Parliament shall have legal force in Nagaland, unless specially applied to it by a majority vote of the Nagaland legislative assembly. On 1 December 1963, Nagaland was officially made the sixteenth state of the Indian Union by merging the Tuensang Frontier Division and the Naga Hills District of Assam. Point seven of the Sixteen Point Agreement was enshrined as Article 371(A) of the Indian Constitution, giving Nagaland a special status where the Nagaland Legislative Assembly has veto power over any law passed in India pertaining to or affecting Nagaland. The Article exempts Nagaland from Indian Government resolutions regarding (1)(a)(i) religious or social practices of the Nagas, (1)(a)(ii) Naga customary law and procedure, (1)(a)(iii) administration of civil and criminal justice involving customary law, (1)(a)(iv) ownership and transfer of land and resources. Furthermore, the Article places special responsibility with respect to law and order in the state of Nagaland in the hands of the Governor of Nagaland. Essentially, Article 371(A) grants specific exclusions to Nagaland from the Constitution of India that effectively entrench a negotiated sovereignty in the state. Under the provision, Nagaland Legislative Assembly can make inapplicable any law passed by Indian Parliament pertaining to the above items. The Article is thus both a compromise on the demands for Naga independence, and an inheritance of decades of differential treatment of the Naga Hills.

Statehood did little to allay conflict. Rather, in the decades following statehood and Article 371(A), myriad insurgent groups formed from splits and divisions of earlier groups and formed from town and village-based movements. Disagreements over the authority to make collectively binding decisions were a significant factor in this factioning. As early as 1957 the Naga National Council (NNC) split along ideological lines between its moderate members, open to dialogue with the government of India, and members following Phizo, opposed to negotiations. Throughout the 1960s and early 1970s, a series of further splits within the NNC and the Naga Federal Government (NFG) took place, largely along tribal lines. In response to rising violence between Naga nationalist factions, the Nagaland Peace Council was founded as a church-led initiative, with aims of persuading underground leaders to take part in peace talks with the Government of India. Five official rounds of talks were attempted between 1968 and 1975, culminating in the Shillong Accord on 11 November 1975, signed between breakaway members of the Naga National Council (NNC) and the Government of India in Shillong in the state of Meghalaya (Das, 2011: 75). Under the Accord, Naga representatives agreed to accept, without condition, the Constitution of India (Shimray, 2005: 102). However, NNC leadership were not present. The Accord thus marked a critical divide within the founding Naga nationalist group, and distinct from earlier divides, it involved a breakaway faction acceding to the demands of the Government of India. In the wake of the Accord, violence between Naga nationalist factions increased dramatically. Violence followed tribal lines, with many pro-Accordist members being from the economically dominant Angami tribe, and anti-Accordist members being a consortium of Konyak, Tangkhulhil, Khiamniungan, Sema, Ao, Mao, and Yimgchunger tribes. Following years of tension and infighting between pro-Accordist and anti-Accordist factions, Isak Chishi Swu, Thuingaleng Muivah and other anti-Accordists sheltering in Myanmar formed the 'National Socialist Council of Nagaland (NSCN)' on 31 January 1980 in the Eastern Naga Hills (Upper Myanmar) to establish a 'People's Republic of Nagaland' inspired by Mao Zedong's communist ideology (Das, 2011: 75). In 1988, the NSCN split following open conflict between Hemi-Konyak Nagas of Burma, allied to S.S. Khaplang, and Tangkhul Nagas of Ukhrul, allied to Isak Chishi Swu and Thuingaleng Muviah. This conflict led to the emergence of the two largest competing nationalist factions in Nagaland today, the National Council of Nagalim under Isak Chishi Swu and Thuingaleng Muviah (NSCN-IM), and the Nationalist Council of Nagalim under S.S. Khaplang (NSCN-K). Fighting between nationalists overlapped with inter-tribal conflicts and clan and family feuds, creating deep fissures in the nationalist movement and increasingly involved targeting civilians who were suspected spies and traitors and public executions of drug dealers and drug users (Kikon, 2017).

In 1991 the Government of India adopted a liberalized export-oriented economic model that depended to a great degree on closer economic and political ties to Asia. From the early 1990s the increasing focus on trade ties to Asia lent new weight and urgency to resolving pervasive conflicts spread throughout Northeast India. The failure of earlier agreements to pacify the Naga insurgency, and the limitations of military campaigns to contain the armed struggle combined with post-liberalization efforts to strengthen ties with Asian trade partners, through Northeast India, compelled the Government of India to engage in new negotiations to end conflict in the Northeast (Longchari, 2016: 240). Ceasefire in Nagaland was a crucial component in these negotiations. The processes leading to this ceasefire began, roughly, in June 1995, when Prime Minister P.V. Narasimha Rao met with Isak Chishi Swu of the NSCN-IM, seeking to resolve the 'Naga problem'[4] through political dialogue rather than military means. In November 1996 Prime Minister H.D. Deve Gowda sent former Union Minister for State, Rajesh Pilot, to meet with NSCN-IM members in Bangkok. Following this meeting, on 3 February 1997 Deve Gowda met with NSCN-IM leaders in Zurich. In August 1997

4   The 'Naga problem' and 'Naga issue' are commonly used terms for Naga insurgency.

the NSCN-IM ceasefire agreement with the Union Government of India was finalized. On 9 April 2000, Nagaland's second largest nationalist group, the NSCN-K, announced its own unilateral ceasefire with the Government of India on near identical terms, with the ceasefire period beginning in 2001.

Ceasefires signed in 1997 and 2001 mark the end of open hostilities between Naga nationalist groups and the Government of India, and the beginning of a complex peace-making process in Nagaland. Ceasefires are occasionally abrogated, re-negotiated, and in some cases abandoned completely. In the wake of ceasefire, Nagaland is a complex amalgamation of sovereign actors including India's paramilitary, the Nagaland State Government, Naga customary institutions, and a number of shadow governments associated with Naga nationalist groups. Naga nationalist groups have multiplied dramatically, with new groups such as the NSCN-KK, NSCN-R, and NSCN-U emerging from factions and splits in the NSCN-IM and NSCN-K. The presence of multiple new insurgent groups and the overlapped and ambiguous nature of sovereignty is met with a degree of tolerance by the central and state governments. This tolerated plurality has been established through ceasefires signed between underground groups and the Government of India, through special provisions in India's Constitution enshrining customary village institutions and authorities, and through selective tolerance of overlapping territorial claims and illegal taxation, creating a tentative peace in the state that is only occasionally disrupted. Simultaneously, Naga customary institutions govern local laws, oversee dispute resolution in towns and villages, and manage the ownership and transfer of land. These institutions differ between tribes, clans, and villages. In smaller towns and villages especially, where Nagaland State Government is less visible, customary institutions function as embodiments of the state. Efforts to place these institutions into a framework for the state has also created ambiguous overlaps between state and customary institutions. The presence of Indian armed forces, paramilitaries, a poorly resourced state government, and customary institutions whose structures and legitimacy differs between urban and rural areas, tribes, clans, and villages has contributed to a complex and ambiguous sovereignty in Nagaland. The result is a dysfunctional governance marked by endemic and widespread corruption, unreliable or absent services, and broken infrastructure.

Conclusion

Nagaland's status as a frontier and contested borderland has roots in its difficult geography and differential treatment under British colonial

administration. Distance, steep and jagged geography, and diverse populations that either settled on fortified mountains or moved often with the
jhum cycle presented immense challenges to colonial state makers. In
efforts to contain and subdue highland communities, various bordering
policies were developed. Some of these, such as the Inner Line Regulations,
continue to hold great relevance today. Following India's independence in
1947, expectations of dramatic political change and independent sovereignty held by many Naga communities were quelled. Separatist pushes in
Nagaland were met with draconian measures by the Indian government.
Indian paramilitaries, the Assam Rifles, were stationed throughout the
Naga Hills District, permanent military camps and bases were established,
and extraordinary laws were enacted in the form of the Armed Forces
Special Powers Act (1958) and the Disturbed Areas Act (1972). In 1963, the
state of Nagaland was formed by combining the Naga Hills District of As-
sam with the Tuensang Frontier Division. Statehood included a special
amendment to India's Constitution, Article 371(A), granting exclusions to
Nagaland from Indian laws and protecting and preserving Naga customary
institutions. Despite statehood and constitutional provisions, conflict in
Nagaland continued, and throughout the 1970s and 1980s divisions in the
Naga nationalist movement resulted in a dramatic increase in internecine
violence in the state and surrounding states. In the 1990s, amid Indian
efforts to liberalize the economy and strengthen connections with Southeast
Asia, resolving insurgent conflict in the Northeast gained new weight and
urgency. A ceasefire was signed between the NSCN-IM and the Government
of India in 1997. Another ceasefire was signed between the NSCN-K and the
Government of India in 2001. While these ceasefires did not end conflict
between Naga nationalist groups, they did mark the beginning of a prolonged
peace-making process in Nagaland and the opening up of the state to greater
political, economic, and cultural connections to India. In the following
chapter, I discuss the ways that decades of armed conflict continue to shape
life in Nagaland, even as the state approaches its third decade of ceasefire.

References

Baruah, S. (2003). 'Confronting constructionism: Ending India's Naga War'. *Journal
    of Peace Research* 40(3): 321–338. DOI: 10.1177/0022343303040003005.
British East India Company (1826). Treaty of Yandabo.
Bruce, R. (1840). 'Mr Bruce's report on Assam tea'. *Chambers' Edinburgh Journal*,
    25 January. Edinburgh.

Brunnschweiler, R.O. (1966). 'On the geology of the Indoburman ranges'. *Journal of the Geological Society of Australia* 13(1): 137–194. DOI: 10.1080/00167616608728608.

Chakravarti, P.C. (1971). *The evolution of India's northern borders*. London: Asia Publishing House. DOI: 10.1017/CBO9781107415324.004.

Changoiwala, P. (2020). 'India's Muslims are terrified of being deported'. *Foreign Policy*, 21 February. Washington D.C.

Dalhousie, J.B. (1851). 'Relations to be maintained with the Angami Nagas'. In: Acharyya, N.N. (ed.) *Historical documents of Assam and neighbouring states: Original records in English*. New Delhi. Omsons.

Das, D. (2014). 'Understanding margins, state power, Space and territoriality in the Naga Hills'. *Journal of Borderlands Studies* 29(1): 63–80. DOI: 10.1080/08865655.2014.892693.

Das, N.K. (2011). 'Naga peace parleys: Sociological reflections and a plea for pragmatism'. *Economic & Political Weekly* 46(25): 70–77.

Dzüvichü, L. (2014). 'Empire on their backs: Coolies in the eastern borderlands of the British Raj'. *International Review of Social History* 59(22): 89–112. DOI: 10.1017/S0020859014000170.

Elwin, V. (1969). *The Nagas in the nineteenth century*. London: Oxford University Press.

Gait, E. (1906). *A history of Assam*. 1st ed. Calcutta: Thacker, Spink & Co.

Gait, E. (1926). *A history of Assam*. 2nd ed. Calcutta: Thacker, Spink & Co.

Government of India (1873). Bengal Eastern Frontier Regulation, 1873.

Government of India (1874). Scheduled District Act XVI of 1874. XVI.

Government of India (1958). The Armed Forces (Assam and Manipur) Special Powers Act, 1958. 28.

Guha, A. (1967). 'Colonisation of Assam: Years of transitional crisis (1825–40)'. In: *Staff Seminar of Gokhale Institute of Politics and Economics*, Poona, 1967.

Guha, A. (1985). *Medieval and early colonial Assam*. Calcutta: K.C. Bagchi.

Haokip, T. (2012). 'Political integration of Northeast India: A historical analysis'. *Strategic Analysis* 36(2): 304–314. DOI: 10.1080/09700161.2012.646508.

Hausing, K.K.S. (2014). 'Asymmetric federalism and the question of democratic justice in Northeast India'. *India Review* 13(2): 87–111. DOI: 10.1080/14736489.2014.904151.

Hutton, J.H. (1921). *The Angami Nagas: With some notes on neighbouring tribes*. London: Macmillan and Co Ltd.

Johnstone, J. (1896). *My experiences in the Manipur and the Naga Hills*. London: Sampson Low, Marston and Company.

Joshi, V. (2007). 'The birth of Christian enthusiasm among the Angami of Nagaland'. *South Asia: Journal of South Asian Studies* 30(3): 541–557. DOI: 10.1080/00856400701714120.

Joshi, V. (2013). 'The micropolitics of borders: The issue of greater Nagaland (or Nagalim)'. In: Gellner, D.N. (ed.) *Borderland lives in northern South Asia*. Durham, NC: Duke University Press.

Kikon, D. (2005). 'Operation Hornbill Festival 2004'. In: *Gateway to the East: Symposium on Northeast India and the Look East Policy*, 2005.

Kotwal, D. (2008). 'The Naga insurgency: The past and the future'. *Strategic Analysis* 24(4): 751–772. DOI: 10.1080/09700160008455245.

Kurtenbach, S. (2012). 'Postwar youth violence: A mirror of the relationship between youth and adult society violence and security'. *GIGA Research Program: Violence and Security*. Hamburg: German Institute of Global Area Studies.

Longchari, A. (2016). *Self determination: A resource for JustPeace*. Dimapur: Heritage Publishing House.

Longkumer, A. (2018a). '"Along Kingdom's Highway": The proliferation of Christianity, education, and print amongst the Nagas in Northeast India'. *Contemporary South Asia* 27(2): 160–178. DOI: 10.1080/09584935.2018.1471041

Longkumer, A. (2018b). 'Bible, guns and land: Sovereignty and nationalism amongst the Nagas of India'. *Nations and Nationalism* 24(4): 1097–1116. DOI: 10.1111/nana.12405.

Mackenzie, A. (1884). *History of the relations of the government with the hill tribes of the north-east frontier of Bengal*. Calcutta: Home Department Press.

Mahanta, N.G. (2013). *Confronting the state: ULFA's quest for sovereignty*. New Delhi: SAGE Publications.

M'Cosh, J. (1837). *Topography of Assam*. Calcutta: G.H. Huttmann Bengal Military Orphan Press.

Mills, J.P. (1935). 'The Naga headhunters of Assam'. *Journal of the Royal Central Asian Society* 22(3): 418–424. DOI: 10.1080/03068373508725375.

Misra, S. (2011). *Becoming a borderland: The politics of space and identity in colonial Northeastern India*. New York: Routledge. DOI: 10.4324/9780203085301.

Naga National Council (1947). Naga-Akbar Hydari Accord (Nine Point Agreement).

Najman, Y., Sobel, E.R., Millar, I. et al. (2020). 'The exhumation of the Indo-Burman Ranges, Myanmar'. *Earth and Planetary Science Letters* 530(15). DOI: 10.1016/j.epsl.2019.115948.

Pemberton, R.B. (1827). 'A singular race of people'. In: Wilson, H.H. (ed.) *Documents illustrative of the Burmese War*. Oxford: Oxford University Press.

Reed, R. (1942). *History of the frontier areas bordering on Assam*. Shillong: Assam Government Press.

Sarmah, B. (2016). 'The cauldron of conflict: Politics of peace, governance and development in India's North-East'. *Social Scientist* 4(11): 15–36.

Scott, J.C. (2009). *The art of not being governed: An anarchist history of upland Southeast Asia*. New Haven: Yale University Press.

Sharma, J. (2011). *Empire's garden: Assam and the making of India*. London: Duke University Press.

Shimray, A.S.A. (2005). *Let freedom ring: Story of Naga nationalism*. New Delhi: Promilla & Co. Publishers.

Singh C (2004). *Naga politics: A critical account*. New Delhi: Mittal Publications.

Superintendent of the Assam Secretariat (1896). *Physical and political geography of the province of Assam*. Shillong: Assam Secretariat Printing Office.

Teron, D. (2014). 'Charhepi's song – Karbi women's funeral lament'. In: Passing things on: Ancestors and genealogies in Northeast India, 103–110.

Thong, T. (2010). '"Thy kingdom come": The impact of colonization and proselytization on religion among the Nagas'. *Journal of Asian and African Studies* 45(6): 595–609. DOI: 10.1177/0021909610373915.

Thong, T. (2012). 'Civilized colonizers and barbaric colonized: Reclaiming Naga identity by demythologizing colonial portraits'. *History and Anthropology* 23(3): 375–397. DOI: 10.1080/02757206.2012.697060.

Times of India (2019). 'Why the northeast is up in arms against the Citizenship Bill'. 13 December. New Delhi.

Times of India (2020). 'CAA to fulfill old promises to religious minorities in neighbouring countries: Modi'. 28 January. New Delhi.

van Schendel, W. (2002). 'A politics of nudity: Photographs of the "Naked Mru" of Bangladesh'. *Modern Asian Studies* 36: 341–374. DOI: 10.1017/S0026749X02002032.

van Schendel, W. (2002b). 'Geographies of knowing, geographies of ignorance: Jumping scale in Southeast Asia'. *Environment and Planning D: Society and Space* 20: 647–668. DOI: 10.1068/d16s.

von Fürer-Haimendorf, C. (1938). *The naked Nagas: Head-hunters of Assam in peace and war*. London: Metuen and Co.

West, A. (1985). 'Nineteenth century Naga material culture'. *Museum Ethnographers Group* 18: 21–34.

West, A. (1994). 'Writing the Nagas: A British officers' ethnographic tradition'. *History and Anthropology* 8(1–4): 55–88. DOI: 10.1080/02757206.1994.9960858.

Wettstein, M. (2012). 'Origin and migration myths in the rhetoric of Naga independence and collective identity'. In: Huber, T. and Blackburn, S. (eds) *Origins and migrations in the extended Eastern Himalayas*. Leiden: Brill, 213–239.

Wilkinson, M. (2017). 'Masculinity in the margins: Men and identity in 21st century Nagaland'. In: Wouters, J.J.P. and Heneise, M. (eds) *Nagas in the 21st century*. Kohima: Highlander Books.

Zou, D.V. (2005). 'Raiding the dreaded past: Representations of headhunting and human sacrifice in north-east India'. *Contributions to Indian Sociology* 39(1): 75–105. DOI: 10.1177/006996670503900103.

3   Legacies of Conflict

Abstract

Chapter 3, 'Legacies of Conflict', discusses the complex legacies of decades
of nationalist conflict that continue in Nagaland, including multiple
sovereign contestants, disagreements over Nagaland's borders with
neighbouring states, and the pervasive presence of an alternative map
for a Naga homeland, 'Nagalim', that challenges India's cartographic
limits. In this complex scenario, a highly masculinized political culture
has emerged, one that encourages 'strongman' politics and an especially
salient gendered social order.

Keywords: post-conflict, militarization, insurgency, trauma

Nagaland Republic Day

22 March 2016 marked the 60th Nagaland Republic Day recognized by
Nagaland's oldest nationalist-insurgent group, the Naga National Council
(NNC). The day celebrates the establishment of the Federal Government
of Nagaland on 22 March 1956. Other Naga nationalist groups celebrate
their own republic days on different dates, marking when their respective
governments were founded. The NNC's Nagaland Republic Day involved an
assembly of supporters at Chedema Peace Camp on the outskirts of Kohima,
the headquarters of the Federal Government of Nagaland. The NNC president
at the time, Viyalie Metha, opened the event with a series of Christian
blessings and prayers, and an extended thanks given to the speakers and
special guests at the occasion. Following the prayer and welcome, Metha
delivered an extended recounting of the difficult circumstances that the
Federal Government of Nagaland was founded in. As with most nationalist
histories of Nagaland, his recounting began with the Naga declaration of
independence on 14 August 1947, and guided the audience through the
hardships and injustices endured by Naga communities at the hands of
Indian paramilitaries in the 1950s, 1960s, and 1970s. The chronological history

Wilkinson, Matthew: *Borderland Anxieties. Shifting Understandings of Gender, Place and Identity
at the India-Burma Border.* Amsterdam: Amsterdam University Press, 2023
DOI: 10.5117/9789463729789_CH03

Figure 2: Assam Rifles camp, Kohima. 2016. Taken by author.

was broken up with occasional mentions of traditional Naga governance systems and references to a 'pure Naga democracy' marked by a vague but widely understood model of village sovereignty, Christian devotion, and independence from outside rule. Metha closed his speech with calls for a resurgence of the nationalist spirit and a reunification of Naga territories outside of the state. The speech was followed by a series of other speeches by prominent NNC leaders, by the nephew of one of the founders of the Naga nationalist movement, the late Angami Zapu Phizo, and by Kaka Iralu, a revered writer and historian of the Naga nationalist movement. All of the speeches followed a familiar and somewhat repetitive format, beginning with prayers and blessings, thanking notable members of the panel and crowd for their presence, presenting a history of Nagaland's conflict with India, and calling for revival of a 'traditional' Naga society and unification with Naga communities residing outside of the state. The event ended with a performance by a troupe of young Naga dancers and a lunch of pork, rice, and local greens. Following the speeches and the lunch, the audience dispersed, and a caravan of Mahindra Bolero four-wheel-drives and small hatchback cars made the tedious journey back to Kohima, navigating the dirt road between the camp and the town. I returned to my hotel in the centre of Kohima mostly disappointed. I had flyers listing the speakers and scribbled notes of the speeches they gave, detailing the same chronological history of Nagaland's nationalist movement that I had been given by almost every other nationalist supporter I had met. It was rich in facts and often impassioned, but nothing new and nothing surprising.

I leant over a table in the hotel lobby making small talk with the hotel staff as I flicked through my notes, looking for anything I had written down that might have offered something new or interesting. The three boys working in the lobby, aged between about fifteen and twenty, asked about the camp and what I thought of the event. None of them had been to Chedema. Not sure if I would offend them, I tried to keep the discussion light and hide my disappointment. I mentioned the history in the speeches and the nationalist movement, trying to prod the boys to offer their opinions of the NNC or the wider nationalist push. The boys were polite and responsive but did not seem very interested. They were much more curious about the road leading to Chedema. They asked if the rough road had made me sick, if I was ever worried that the car would fall off the side of the mountain, and if we had roads like that in Australia. Our conversation ended abruptly when the power went out. Two of the boys went to start the generator, while the other left to check on the kitchen.

I left the hotel and proceeded on my regular habit of walking along National Highway 2 (NH2), past Kohima's famous Second World War cemetery, uphill towards BOC, an intersection close to the police headquarters, that is named after the Burma Oil Company station that used to be at the site. BOC was a reliable source of some of the cheapest street-food in Kohima, was close to a bookshop that had more reliable internet than the hotel, and the walk uphill provided views of most of the city. The walk to BOC starts at another acronym-named site, NST, in the centre of the city. NST is a crowded and loud part of Kohima named after the Nagaland State Transport station that is located in its centre. The rapid construction of multi-storey shopping complexes in the central street over the past five years, where before there were single-story, dark wood supply stores, has narrowed the footpath to the point that in many parts pedestrians are forced onto the road. Where there is available space to walk, shopfronts overflow into the street, creating an obstacle course of cathode ray TVs, children's toys, and stacked shoeboxes.

The road itself is potholed and muddy, a result of poor maintenance and the heavy vehicles and busses that are filtered through NST. Leaving the crowded footpath altogether means navigating deep puddles, oil slicks and traffic. It is a vibrant and fun part of the city, but tedious and frustrating to move through.

Avoiding NST, I chose to walk behind the hotel, through the Kohima's near permanently muddy football field and a maze of small alleyways behind the Assam Rifles camp near the centre of the city. The camp itself is immense, with high walls and barbed wire fences effectively partitioning the centre of the city. Along the camp's walls, posters feature images of Assam Rifles paramilitaries providing medical assistance to elderly Nagas, handing out satellite dishes, and proclaiming the Assam Rifles' contributions to security and wellbeing in the state. The posters are all marked with the phrase 'Assam Rifles, Friends of the Hill Peoples'. Rusted barbed wire fencing peaks over the top of the camp walls with liquor bottles tied together at regular points that jingle when the wire is touched. As Nagaland has officially been a dry state since 1989, the bottles were a conspicuous addition to the fence and reminder, whether deliberate or accidental, that the armed forces are not held to the same rules and laws as the communities they patrol.

As I passed the camp, a convoy of heavily armed Assam Rifles paramilitaries packed into Suzuki-Maruti Gypsy jeeps raced by and turned onto NH2 ahead, moving towards NST. The convoy members wore black balaclavas and towels wrapped around their faces as they drove through, a practical way of protecting their eyes and faces from the dust and small rocks that are inevitably kicked up when driving on the poorer-maintained sections of Kohima's roads. When the convoy reached the traffic at NST, they honked until cars and trucks moved to each side of the road to let them pass. This is a daily event in Kohima, a frustrating but predictable and banal part of life in the city. Nobody else stopped to watch the convoy pass through.

Standing up-hill, half-way to BOC, I was able to pause to look back at the busy central street, the muddy football field, and the maze of small alleyways I had cut through earlier. To the left of my gaze, NH2 extended along a high ridge, towards Kohima Village, where the original Angami settlement stood, and continued on to High School Junction, what many consider to be the last point of 'main' Kohima and the beginning of the city's outskirts. Along the road were narrower streets of wood and brick houses with rusted corrugated iron rooftops and spires of the various tribal-affiliated churches in the city – Kohima Ao Baptist Church, Sumi Baptist Church, Sumi Aphuyemi Baptist Church, and the Christian Revival Mission Church. To the right, the Assam Rifles camp with its distinct white walls extended downhill.

The camp was dotted with pastel yellow concrete apartment blocks for housing the officers and their families. There were satellite dishes and a radio tower, well-manicured lawns and tiered gardens. There was a school in the camp for the children of the officers, a grassed and mown soccer field, and a helipad on the camp's eastern boundary. Women in saris could be seen walking the grounds of the camp and hanging laundry along the outside of the apartment blocks. The immense camp resembled a city of its own, growing out of the side of Kohima, but a complete contrast to Kohima.

These observations in the centre of Kohima are telling of the complex and often subtle peace-conflict dynamics taking place in Nagaland in the wake of decades of ceasefire. On the one hand, the state's conflict is largely ended, and the idea of an independent and sovereign 'Nagalim' is seen as archaic to many Nagas. The style of militant nationalism embodied in the NNC and various other nationalist insurgent groups holds little relevance to younger Nagas, for whom long rallies and remembrance days are dull, and the idea of jungle fighting against Indian armed forces is difficult to even imagine. Rather, life in Nagaland is increasingly urbanized and connected. Satellite TV, mobile phone services and high-speed internet, while not always reliable, are widespread in the state's larger urban areas and increasingly found in smaller towns as well. In larger towns especially, a growing post-conflict economy has brought goods and services from all over the world, and locally grown produce is sold alongside second-hand Korean clothes, Japanese whitegoods, and Indian electronics. Essentially, life in Nagaland reflects that of most other growing and urbanizing places, marked by widely available consumer goods and services, the background noise of constant construction projects, and the frustrations of crowded footpaths and traffic.

Yet, simultaneously, signs of militarization, conflict, and of living at the 'edges' of the state are everywhere. Nationalist insurgent groups hold permanent camps on the outskirts of large towns, not just the NNC's Chedema Peace Camp outside Kohima, but also the NSCN-IM's 'Camp Hebron' on the outskirts of Dimapur, the NSCN-U's headquarters in Dimapur, and numerous other smaller camps run by gangs, village guards and vigilante groups spread throughout the state and along the India/Burma border. Most towns and cities have military checkpoints at town entries, while others are placed along larger roads and at intersections, where people are forced to identify themselves and often asked about where they are coming from and where they are going to, and where people can be forced out of their vehicles and searched for weapons or other contraband without justification. The permanent military presence, along with impunities granted to Indian paramilitaries under AFSPA encourages an environment of constant risk. Interactions between locals and paramilitaries are fraught with anxiety and a sense that anything can happen. Shootings of civilians by Indian paramilitaries, sometimes accidental and sometimes deliberate, often referred to as 'crossfire killings', continue even after official ceasefire. Many discussants mentioned that crossfire killings and other incidents of extreme state violence were common although often went unreported, especially in rural and isolated villages. Overall, life is lived under the close watch of a highly visible and invasive military-state apparatus that acts with almost complete impunity. Even seemingly banal items, such as liquor bottles hanging on barbed wire, send a conspicuous message that the armed forces that people pass and are forced to interact with every day operate outside of and above Naga society and state law. In other parts of the country, nationalist insurgent groups and vigilantes do not hold camp outside major cities, convoys of heavily armed and masked paramilitaries do not patrol city streets, ambushes and gunfights are not common events, and everyday items like hanging bottles do not tell stories of power and impunity. These things only happen in unusual, sensitive, and peripheral places.

This chapter marks the final chapter of Part 1 of the book, discussing how periphery is made, remade, and experienced in Nagaland. The previous chapter discussed the various ways Nagaland has become a frontier, a 'backward tract', and a borderland. Associations of periphery underpin all of these designations. However, as I argue in this chapter, periphery is more than a designation. Where spaces are imagined and constructed as frontiers, approached as backward tracts or scheduled spaces, and divided as borderlands, periphery is experienced. People live with a sense of being at a periphery, outside of and away from the state and the order that is associated with the state-centre. This sense of periphery is amplified by Nagaland's ongoing militarization and the legacies of decades of armed conflict in the state, in the form of exceptional laws applied to the state, dysfunctional infrastructure and corrupt governance, the presence of multiple armed insurgent groups, and a population of post-combatants who find themselves at the fringes of a post-conflict borderland state.

Militarization, Exception and Periphery

The territory that is Nagaland today has, arguably, always been governed according to security imperatives. Before the colonial encounter, communities living in the highlands settled on high ground and built complex systems of fences and traps to guard against raids from other tribes (Johnstone, 1896). Relations between tribes involved periods of tension and conflict, and governance often relied on building alliances and systems of tribute between tribes (Owen, 1844: 84). Colonial administration, likewise, focused on first avoiding and second controlling political tensions in the Naga Hills (Johnstone, 1896: 40). The boundaries of the Naga Hills District were initially drawn at the Naga foothills as a security response to the risk of Naga raids on foothill tea plantations, and colonial governors had almost all come from military backgrounds (West, 1994). The present capital, Kohima, an otherwise inconvenient and poorly serviced mountaintop village that is prone to landslides and has poor access to water, was chosen over more connected sites such as Chümoukedima and Wokha because of its superior vantage for military expeditions (Johnstone, 1896: 50). Even the migration of Marwari traders in the Naga Hills, one of the few groups who were encouraged to move and settle beyond the Inner Line, was to provide supply lines for British military expeditions (Dzüvichü, 2014). However, following India's independence, securitizing the Naga Hills took on new significance. From 1947, the Assam Police were brought into the state to subdue demands for independent sovereignty. Following the Naga plebiscite in 1951, where 99 per cent of Nagas voted in favour of independent sovereignty for the Naga Hills, this military presence increased dramatically, and permanent Assam Rifles camps were established throughout the state. From 11 September 1958 the Armed Forces Special Powers Act (AFSPA) was applied in the Naga Hills and Tuensang Frontier districts. The AFSPA applies to areas deemed 'disturbed' by the Government of India. 'Disturbed status' may be granted in any area where an 'extensive disturbance of the public peace and tranquillity, by reason of differences or disputes between members of different religion, racial, language or regional groups or castes or communities' (Disturbed Areas (Special Courts) Act (1976)). 'Disturbed' status is a self-perpetuating cycle. As argued by Kikon (2009: 273), 'the AFSPA marks the Northeast [India] as a "disturbed area" and its people as "suspicious" ... these categories reproduce each other, so that the area inhabited by suspicious persons will evidently become a disturbed area, and those inhabiting a disturbed area fall under suspicion'. Once an area is deemed 'disturbed', AFSPA gives practical impunity to Indian armed forces in the area, granting extreme discretion to armed forces in their operations against real and perceived insurgent groups (Baruah, 2014: 3). The AFSPA enables the emergence and continuation of what Sanjib Baruah refers to as 'a parallel political structure that works outside the rules and norms that govern India's democratic political institutions' (2007: 61).

Adding to a sense of invasion, the Indian paramilitaries that committed these acts often looked distinctly different from Nagas, did not speak
any local dialects or Nagamese, and represented a hegemonic and hyper-
nationalistic Indian culture that was considered to be at odds with local
customs and cultural norms. Highlighting these differences, one former
combatant discussing his own motivations for 'going underground'[1] detailed
his experiences being stopped and checked while growing up in a smaller
town in Nagaland:

> Back home, whenever we came back home, whenever we came back home
> we suddenly felt different ... Indian guys are checking us in our land. Know
> what I mean? Suppose in our village gate, nobody is supposed to ask me
> who I am, everybody is supposed to know, but a black guy[2] comes and
> asks me, I'm not being racist here, a foreigner comes and asks, 'Who the
> Hell are you?' How would you feel? That sort of thing gets implanted in
> my mind when I was a kid and so I ask dad, why are they asking us who
> we are, don't they know this is our village, not their village?

Militarization and its associated violence was and continues to be especially
gendered. Some discussants argued that this was systematic, aimed at
humiliating and degrading Naga women and emasculating Naga men by
undermining their abilities to protect the women around them. Harassment
by armed paramilitaries continues to be common, and several discussants have described interactions at stop-checks involving empowered and
domineering Indian soldiers leering into vehicles and making suggestive and
sexual comments about female passengers. In light of the gendered violence,
and the traditional association between men and fighter/guardian roles in
Naga traditions, Naga men were placed at the forefront of the struggle to
protect Naga territory, culture, and society from the incursions and abuses of
Indian paramilitaries. The Naga nationalist struggle involved the emergence
and promotion of a hyper-masculine Naga nationalist movement that stood
at odds with the occupying Indian hegemon and reified men's self-styled
roles as guardians and protectors, in many ways reflecting traditional men's
roles in Naga communities as fighters and village defenders. The Naga

1   A common phrase used to describe joining a Naga insurgent group
2   'Black' was often used by discussants to refer to Indian soldiers and Indians living in Nagaland.
While in many contexts, 'black' has racist connotations and is considered offensive, when
raised in my own interviews, 'black' was employed by participants as a metonym for Indian,
highlighting the physical distinctions between Nagas and Indians.

Freedom Fighter, otherwise referred to as the Naga National Worker, was mythicized and popularized in Naga literature as the masculine embodiment of nationalist duties to oppose the Indian military occupation and liberate Nagaland from outsider encroachments (see Iralu, 2009: 218, for the most explicit example). Throughout the conflict, conversions to Christianity accelerated dramatically, with Nagas identifying as Christian, typically Evangelical or Baptist, growing from 18 per cent in 1941 to 80 per cent in 1981 (Longkumer, 2018a: 10). Christianity provided Naga converts with a coherent distinction from the Hindu-nationalism of Indian paramilitaries, a distinction that was more recognizable than the many tribe-specific animist faiths (Thong, 2010: 599). Christian family models and patriarchal Biblical dogmas also presented Naga converts with a rigidly gendered social order that translated well into tribal patriarchal traditions, tied to men and women having pre-destined roles and spaces in nuclear family structures, church customs, and public life (Hausing, 2018: 261).

Naga nationalist groups were and are overwhelmingly male in their membership and masculine in their ideologies, linking male-dominated customary institutions with rigidly gendered Christian traditions that involve men as leaders and guardians, and women as followers and in need of guardianship (Longkumer, 2018b). While women did take part in the Naga conflict as well, and Nagaland's larger nationalist groups, the NSCN-IM and the NSCN-K have actively encouraged women to join their ranks for decades (Banerjee, 1999: 138), women's activities in Naga nationalist groups typically reflected rigid gender norms that reappear throughout Naga society. As Gill (2005: iv) clarifies, 'these women worked as informers, bearers of loads and rations, cooking and sheltering [male] cadres as even among rebel groups the duties of men and women vary ... they often find themselves trapped into doing the same chores and household jobs that they would ordinarily take on in their homes'. With few, but some exceptions, women's involvement in Nagaland's conflict has been limited to two forms: either as victims of sexual violence at the hands of Indian paramilitaries (Kikon, 2015), or as peace-promoters, conforming to understandings of women as mothers, carers, and peacemakers (Bora, 2017). Essentially, the gendered nature of militarization and conflict in Nagaland itself reproduced an ideology that conflict and public life were the realm of men, while limiting women's movements and involvement in public life to being carers or victims of outsider aggression. This rigidly gendered order was further embedded by attempts to compromise Naga calls for independent sovereignty. Constitutional guarantees of protecting customary laws and institutions, in the form of Article 371(A), endorsed and preserved men's dominance in politics and decision-making in the state (Changkija, 2017; Manchanda and Kakran, 2017). In this sense, Militarization, resistance, and the cultures surrounding the conflict further embedded rigid gender norms in Nagaland, and reified ideas of Naga men as guardians of Naga territory, culture and society.

Since the ceasefire era began, however, Nagaland's nationalist push has fragmented into a collection of warring factions. While factioning and fragmentation are not exclusively a ceasefire phenomenon, a widespread and accelerated unravelling of the Naga nationalist push has taken place since the 1997 and 2001 ceasefires (Kolås, 2011). Prolonged ceasefire in Nagaland is marked by even more divisions between nationalist groups, a further de-centralization of the nationalist push, a further expansion of extractive regimes, and a general fall in the support of the public. Panwar (2017) identifies three splits in the nationalist push since 1997: In 2007, the NSCN-Unification (NSCN-U) was formed by Azheto Chopy, Akhoota Choppy, Khekiye Sumi, and Nukki Sumi and 200 former NSCN-IM cadres. In June 2011, Kitovi Zhimomi, Khole Konyak, and Azheto Chopy split from NSCN-K to form NSCN-Khole Kitovi (NSCN-KK) along with 500 former NSCN-K members. In 2015 the NSCN-K was split again as the NSCN (Reformation) was formed by Wangtin Konyak and P. Tikhak along with 200 former members of the NSCN-K based in Chakhesang District, with some members in Wokha district. However, within each new faction there are also less formal loyalties and networks, sub-factions, and renegade members (Cline, 2006). There are also smaller local militias and village defence organizations, vigilantes and other armed groups active along the Nagaland/Assam border, the Nagaland/Manipur border, and the Nagaland/Myanmar border that claim some degree of legitimacy through Article 371(A) of the Indian Constitution (Wouters, 2017). Many of these groups constitute only a handful of locals as their members (Wouters 2018).

These new nationalist groups have a diverse array of intentions, but are overall less persuasive on the issue of Naga independent sovereignty than their parent-organizations were. Their activities seem to be more focused on securing territory in which to tax communities and controlling roads to toll vehicles on. Essentially, there are now more Naga nationalist groups than at any time during the conflict, and members of these groups are widely perceived to be criminals and extortionists rather than freedom fighters. Once revered Naga nationalist workers are now themselves sources of insecurity. Ao (2013: x) describes this shift aptly: 'Nagaland's story of the struggle for self-determination started with high idealism and romantic notions of fervent nationalism, but it somehow got re-written into one of disappointment and disillusionment because it became the very thing it sought to overcome'. As I detail below, this disappointment and disillusionment is not from a general lack of support for Naga independence, or Naga unification, though that support is waning. Rather, the criminal turn of many insurgent groups, as well as the fracturing and factioning of the nationalist movement has become a new source of insecurity, cost, and frustration for the Naga community.

Serving Smoked Pork to 'Thugs'

> They take 25 per cent of my earnings when I've got customers. If I don't [have customers], they'll come, eat, not cause trouble, and leave. Sometimes they bring guns, but I always give them what they ask. I usually don't allow alcohol in my restaurant. If they get drunk they do mischief.

In June 2012 I came to Noah's restaurant looking for cheap food and an escape from incessant traffic noise in the street. Noah emerged from the kitchen to greet me. Outside of the tourist season in December few tourists come to the restaurant, so my presence provided an unexpected break for Noah from sweeping the kitchen. Noah served smoked pork with rice and sat with me while we drank Zothu (rice wine) from his home village. In 2016 I returned to Noah's restaurant, again outside of the tourist season, and again Noah came to greet me as a break from the general chores of the restaurant. He recognized me and rushed back into the kitchen to collect a bottle of his home village's Zothu. We sat in the empty restaurant and ate smoked pork while I told him about my time in Nagaland after our first meeting, what I had been doing since, and what I was back in Nagaland for. It was a social visit, but I noticed some of the paraphernalia around the restaurant suggested Noah or his staff may have been supporters of the Naga nationalist cause – small Nagalim flags and stickers bearing the common phrase 'Nagaland for Christ'. While other restaurants and businesses occasionally had a blue Nagalim flag or bore a 'Nagaland for Christ' sticker, Noah's restaurant had a lot more paraphernalia than other businesses I had been to. I suspected Noah, as a small business owner, probably also had to pay taxes to the national cause from time to time, whether he supported the nationalist movement or not, which would involve interacting with Naga national workers. Leading up to the visit, I had been spending time with members of Naga nationalist groups and civil society actors and took the opportunity to ask about Noah's experiences with these groups.

Noah was apprehensive to go into detail about his interactions with nationalist groups and the Naga underground but expressed mixed feelings about the nationalist cause. As Noah described it, underground members had been coming to his restaurant for years, even though Noah had opened the restaurant after the ceasefires. In the first few years, men from one of the nationalist groups would come, eat for free, and ask for a contribution to the national cause. Noah said that although he did not like them carrying guns or drinking alcohol[3] in the restaurant, he supported the cause and they generally did not cause much trouble. For Noah, these men represented the ongoing push for Naga unity and nationhood, a cause he was happy to contribute to. However, as myriad groups have emerged in the ceasefire era, Noah's patience and support has worn thinner. Visits by groups occurred more frequently and demands for donations increased, with tax collectors often lifting their shirts when asking for donations to surreptitiously reveal gun hilts and knife handles. Noah also mentioned that occasionally men came into the restaurant openly carrying weapons and threatening violence for payment. At least once, Noah said that national workers had threatened his family and staff directly. Despite these experiences, Noah emphasized his support for what he saw as a genuine push for Naga sovereignty, adamantly mentioning the importance of Naga sovereignty and independence. However, when pressed about whether he believed this sovereignty could be achieved, which I phrased as a 'free Naga homeland', Noah clarified that a lot had to change before that was possible. In light of ongoing ceasefire and the disintegration of a once strong nationalist front, sovereignty in the sense of an independent Naga homeland appears increasingly unlikely. Nationalists coming and demanding money, while they represented the dimming push for some version of Naga sovereignty, could not and would not deliver that sovereignty. The men demanding free food and contributions were extortionists first, and nationalists second.

Noah's experiences being held up by multiple insurgent groups is increasingly common since ceasefires were signed. Similar experiences were recounted by other shopkeepers in Kohima and Dimapur, who described the increasingly violent means used to extract 'donations' and 'taxes' since newer nationalist groups have emerged. Discussants were often hesitant to discuss the men who collect taxes on behalf of Naga nationalist groups in-depth, and this may have been out of concern for being targeted by groups or individuals or may have been due to the stress and anxiety involved in

3   Although rice wine and rice beer are alcoholic, it is common in Nagaland to distinguish traditional alcoholic drinks such as Zothu from imported spirits such as rum and scotch, which are often referred to distinctly as 'alcohol'.

revisiting experiences of being threatened and intimidated into giving donations. What was made clear, however, was that men who collect illegal taxes today were perceived to be different in their ideologies and intentions from the Naga freedom fighters discussed by older Nagas. As the ceasefires continued, albeit interrupted by violence from time to time, the independent sovereignty these groups had initially staked their actions on had become less realistic and less widely supported, and the men visiting his shop were increasingly thug-like. Underground members either leave notes at business doors overnight demanding contributions, or demand contributions on-the-spot and out-of-the-till as businesses are closing at the end of the day. Many discussants speculated that the funds these groups and their members collect are diverted directly to the leadership of nationalist groups to pay for the opulent lifestyles of a conflict-economy elite. It was also common for discussants to surmise that men who do join nationalist groups today do so because they do not want to work or cannot find employment in legitimate activities. Several discussants mentioned that they believed nationalist extortionists were often drug addicts, older unemployed men, or were 'non-locals' who were uneducated or did not have skills to find legitimate forms of employment.

This does not suggest that support for Naga nationalism itself has waned. Rather, this suggests that current Naga national groups are considered to have diverged from the original nationalist cause. As groups have multiplied, and as the Naga community have had to accept overlapping demands to fund these groups, everyday discussions of insurgency draw a clear distinction between a first generation of 'Naga freedom fighters', who taxed communities but presented a somewhat legitimate push for Naga sovereignty, and the rent-seeking partisan nationalists that have emerged since the late 1990s. These newer nationalist workers are widely viewed as extortionists and as profiteering from the ongoing political tensions in the state. Longchari (2016: 243) notes 'with the number of stakeholders increasing in the Naga situation, the conflict has become an industry where various state and non-state groups try to extend the conflict for their own benefit'. Funding comes from diverse sources, including smuggling operations, grafting from state budgets and development projects, and kidnapping. The majority of funding, however, is from illegal taxation operations (Kashypa, 2014). As Ao (2002) argues, 'it is reported that many Naga underground people are now enjoying the most luxurious life in urban areas [after they] returned from the jungle'. Likewise, Bendangjungshi (2011: 68) argues that 'in the name of Naga sovereignty, they use better cars, buy better houses, and live in better conditions'. Imchen's (2017) interview with Tiajungla Soya, a former NNC cadre, similarly reports that 'at present they (people in the underground) join because they are lazy and do not want to work at home'.

This also does not suggest that young people do not join Naga nationalist groups. Young people do continue to join the insurgency. While membership numbers and statistics on enlistment are self-reported, rough, and the number of actual members of these groups is hard to reliably ascertain (Cline, 2006), the evidence that young people are continuing to join Naga nationalist groups is visible. Camps such as the NNC's Chedema Peace Camp, the NSCN-IM's Camp Hebron outside of Dimapur, and smaller local camps and dormitories frequented by insurgent members at Kiphire and Mon Town, contain young members. Young people are often arrested for collecting illegal taxes on behalf of insurgent groups, and young people continue to get abducted, maimed, and killed as members and associates of groups. However, the popular perception of these groups has changed. Within the Naga community groups are less popular and members are looked upon with increasing suspicion, and ceasefire marks a point where insurgency has become a less heroic and less celebrated path that some young people take. This speaks to the divisions of aspirations and possibilities that are emerging and expanding in the post-conflict era, a phenomenon not limited to Nagaland.

That ethno-nationalist movements fragment into warring factions following peace agreements is well established (Farrelly, 2009). This is especially the case in ethno-homeland conflicts in the highlands along the India/ Myanmar and Bangladesh/Myanmar borders (Wilkinson, 2015). These conflicts have roots in overlapping demands for recognition and autonomy by myriad ethnic groups who share a common enemy in the form of the postcolonial state, but otherwise have distinct language, cultures, and histories (Kolås, 2017; Mohaiemen, 2010). As peace agreements have been signed, many signatory groups have divided on the terms of ceasefire, and several autonomy and independence pushes have devolved into factional turf-wars, involving fewer engagements with encroaching state armies and structures, closer entanglements with plains economies and cultures, and increasing violence and predatory extraction by ethno-insurgent groups against local communities (Panwar, 2017). The presence of myriad rivalling Naga factions also encourages cultures of impunity, enabling government officials to graft from development funds under the guise of paying underground taxes, a phenomenon Wouters (2018) refers to as the 'underground effect' – where underground actors such as criminal networks and insurgents operate in conjunction with the existing state framework, laying claim to its resources and funnelling state resources towards nationalist shadow governments that nationalist workers report to (Wouters, 2018).

'There's a big gap in my life, hard to fill'

John was unemployed and spent most of his time either drinking cheap rum or looking for money to buy rum when I met him. His last few years had been especially difficult. John had joined the Naga nationalist struggle straight out of high school in the mid-1990s. At the time, young Naga men especially in Nagaland's interior had limited options for the future. In many interior towns this continues to be the case, although a trend of younger Nagas moving to larger urban areas has meant that being born and raised in a smaller town is less limiting than it once was. In John's case, having failed the public service exam, the options were to either stay at home and farm with his family or join a Naga nationalist group. Joining the nationalist group gave John a sense of accomplishment. As he tells it, his peers praised his decision, and he gained a sense of camaraderie with his fellow cadres. As an organized parallel government, the group presented opportunities to climb ranks, take on more responsibilities, and earn more money, a benefit that even the public service in Nagaland has struggled to provide for many of its workers. Following an injury, John's scope of abilities within the group shrank significantly, and eventually he was unable to continue to work in the group. Now approaching middle age, John has fought in the name of a popular insurgency and had earned success and acceptance in his fighting years. However, John has come overground[4] into a post-conflict society where his alliances in the underground meant little for getting a job, finding a place to live, and meeting people outside of the group. This has been a difficult and emasculating journey, involving moving back in with his parents, struggling with alcohol and drug abuse, post-traumatic stress, and increasing isolation as old ties to the underground are cut, and the few friends he had on the outside grew tired of his drinking and borrowing money. In his own words,

> I can't look for a job, nah. What do I say? I mean, there's nothing I can say though. There's a gap nah? From when I graduated what did you do? I was in the bloody underground ... You can't say that nah. No experience, no nothing ... that's basically the thing, there's a big gap in my life, hard to fill.

4   Left the underground group.

I have no support from outside, nah, support in social media sometimes,
I can write articles, but I don't even have a proper job … It's embarrassing
sometimes, but no other option, no job, nothing. So it's frustration on
frustration, but they're calling me back. I don't know how to answer
them. If I go back, I know, I'll be put back into that regimented space,
nah, where I won't be able to say what I like.[5]

Since coming overground, John has eked out an existence in the outer suburbs
of Kohima. He has attempted to get work through friends; however, as several
mutual friends have informed me, his drinking habits have often led to offers
for work fizzling out, or his quick dismissal from work. In John's own words:

So either I open a business or do something like that, that's all I can do.
And then the problem with me is money. I have no control over money. I
just cannot hold money in my hands. I've held money. I mean, I've been
in charge of huge amounts of money in my life, OK. Huge, huge amounts.
Not [inaudible]. But I never kept it with me. I've been in charge. But I never
keep it with me. Someone else carries it. Cause I know I don't know how
to use the money. It's there one minute in the pocket, next minute it's
gone. I know where I spent it. I know I drink it.
      (Why do you think?)
I mean, it's just all bullshit. It's suddenly gone. That's why I'm scared of
opening a business. Unless I get a good partner who can handle money
well. He gives me pocket money a bit, then handles the rest.
      (What will you do next then?)
Nothing, nothing in my mind. (inaudible). Thing is, the talks nah. If you
can shut this … [recording ended]

When asked about his future plans, John discussed the upcoming negotiations between one of the larger Naga nationalist groups and the Government
of India. He has been overground and outside of the group for nearly a
decade; however, John seemed to be transfixed on the idea that his future
was largely determined by the success or failure of negotiations between the
Government of India and several larger Naga nationalist groups. It seemed
doubtful that these negotiations would affect John in any material sense,
and as several mutual connections made clear, there was no prospect of
John coming back to the underground or being otherwise attached to the

5   In Nagamese, and when many Nagas speak English, 'nah' is used as a discourse market or
'filler word', in the same way that 'like' is often used in American-English speech.

group. However, after so long being involved in an insurgent group, and then coming out of that group into a world with few prospects, a lot of problems, and the stigma and paranoia that underground life often leads to, insurgency and underground life is something familiar, something that John knows he can do. As he describes it, years spent living in the jungle, and travelling throughout India and across borders either illegally or to carry out tasks set by the group, cannot be written on a CV or job application. John's personal history and the ways people in the community can identify him have thus compounded his difficulties finding work. In an insular society like Naga society, where people are often known through several mutual connections in tribes, clans and families, it is easy for John to be 'outed' as a former combatant. As several mutual connections pointed out, his associations with the underground are widely known. While some higher-ranking members of nationalist groups have leveraged their positions and connections with the underground to secure government contracts and build significant wealth, lower ranking members, including John, are more often associated with predatory violence within the Naga community, such as extorting Naga business owners and running illegal road tolls. This has added to a sense that former combatants are unwanted and unwelcome. Hence, leveraging his connections to the underground may be more harmful than helpful in John's case. Unemployment, and the difficulties securing employment following involvement in an insurgent group, committing violence in one's own community, and years spent drinking, has relegated John to the outskirts of both the underground and the overground, with few dependable connections in either. Essentially, the issue is not only that a lack of prospects has led John to joining the underground, but that the time spent in the underground limited John's prospects.

Discussions of men in conflict and post-conflict contexts tend to conflate violence, militaries, dominance, and hegemony, and assume that hegemonic masculinity is embodied in the most violent and most dominant men (Myrttinen et al., 2017: 107, 108). This conflation is part of a wider misunderstanding in the masculinities literature, highlighted by Connell (2005) and Messerschmidt (2019), where 'hegemony' in masculinity is often attributed to masculine traits which are most dominant, most violent, and/or most exaggerated. Second, as Ní Aoláin, Cohn, and Haynes (2016: 235) argue, discussions of masculinity in post-conflict contexts 'fails to account for the many ways that hyper-masculization inherent in hostilities continue to affect societies and underestimates [after conflict] ... [and] the ways in which pre-existing conceptions of masculinity influence the transition process ... Thus, while armed conflict between combatants may end as a result of a peace treaty or ceasefire agreement, violence may remain a persistent feature of the social and cultural landscape of post-conflict societies'.

Research into the generational effects of conflict transformations is also limited. Discussions of post-conflict youth typically portray young men in particular in one of two ways. On the one hand, young men are at-risk of resuming conflicts if not provided with adequate support in the form of education, training, and employment programs (Kurtenbach, 2012; Urdal, 2006). On the other hand, young men, and youth overall are peacemakers and agents of change who are well positioned to lead reconciliation efforts and contribute to resilient post-war communities (Hromadžic, 2015; Schwartz, 2010; Wollentz et al., 2019). Izzi (2013: 103) describes the positioning of youth in discussions of post-conflict as 'alternatively referred to as a "force for peace" or a "threat to peace"'. Overall, discussions of youth and post-conflict portray youth as closely engaged and involved with conflict, the causes of conflict, and the legacies of conflict, whether that engagement involves contributing to conflict or resolving conflict. Here, I adopt an alternative perspective. Younger Nagas interviewed in this research often had little interest in nationalist conflict, or in reconciliation and post-conflict justice. Rather, the younger Nagas I interviewed, had discussions with, and had focus-group sessions with were disengaged from the state's conflict. For Nagas growing up in the era following ceasefire, conflict and its legacies are experienced every day, in the form of seeing Indian paramilitaries patrolling towns and cities, being denied access to large parts of cities and towns that house army camps and barracks, being forced to pay higher prices for goods and services from businesses that have to pay extortive illegal taxes, and in some cases knowing relatives or friends who are members of Naga nationalist groups. However, the Nagas I met with and discussed with were less concerned with and involved in conflict, and more focused on building livelihoods either in the post-conflict economy or outside of Nagaland altogether. Aspirations and goals were attached to getting education and qualifications, finding work, travelling, and building livelihoods in a context of exception and conflict, but delinked from conflict. As Utas (2012) argues, it is most often 'Big Men', influential and elite actors empowered through conflict, who take part in this exclusionary state and market capture. For others, 'small men', who lack such connections, exclusion and marginalization is magnified. Maringira and Carrasco (2015) find that these 'small men' are often ex-combatants but were unable to capture economies, utilize their connections, or otherwise become 'Big Men'. It is these small men who struggle to secure lucrative niches of the state and the market, while also lacking the cultural capital to take part in emerging post-conflict economies, where employability is a central concern (2015).

Conclusion

Despite the signing of ceasefires in the late 1990s and early 2000s, Nagaland continues to host the legacies of decades of armed conflict. Militarization and the presence of a hyper-modern Indian armed presence in the state exists alongside and in stark contrast to the state's poorly resourced infrastructure and dysfunctional civil government institutions. Naga nationalist groups, vigilantes and other armed groups continue to exist and are increasingly associated with crime, illegal taxes, and corruption. Former nationalist workers find themselves isolated and lost in the wake of ceasefire as they navigate long gaps in their work histories, few relevant skills outside of the Nationalist movement, and the stigma associated with having committed violence within their own communities. The presence of these conflict dynamics serves as a reminder that Nagaland is a tense borderland state, a periphery where different laws apply to armed forces and civilians, where multiple sovereign actors vie for control and legitimacy, and where the interrupted and slow end to decades of conflict involves the emergence or at least the expansion of borderland anxieties, politics, and marginalities.

References

Ao, L. (2002). *From Phizo to Muivah: The Naga national question in North-East India*. New Delhi: Mittal Publications.

Ao, T. (2013). *These hills called home: Stories from a war zone*. Dimapur: Zubaan Books.

Banerjee, P. (1999) 'The Naga women's interventions for peace'. *Canadian Woman Studies* 19(4): 137–142.

Baruah, S. (2007). *Durable disorder: Understanding the politics of Northeast India*. New Delhi: Oxford University Press. DOI: 10.1093/acprof:oso/9780195690828.001.0001.

Baruah, S. (2014). 'Routine emergencies: India's Armed Forces Special Powers Act'. In: *Civil war and sovereignty in South Asia: Regional and political economy perspectives*. New Delhi: SAGE Publications.

Bendangjungshi (2011). *Confessing Christ in the Naga context: Towards a liberating ecclesiology*. Zurich: Lit Verlag.

Bora, P. (2017). 'Politics of difference in the northeast: A feminist reflection'. In: Saikia, Y. and Baishya, A.R. (eds) *Northeast India: A place of relations*. Cambridge: Cambridge University Press

Changkija, M. (2017). 'Pride as well as prejudice'. *The Hindu*, 30 May. New Delhi.

Cline, L.E. (2006). 'The insurgency environment in Northeast India'. *Small Wars & Insurgencies* 17(February 2015): 126–147. DOI: 10.1080/09592310600562894.

Connell, R. (2005). *Masculinities*. 2nd ed. New York: Allen & Unwin.

Das, D. (2017). 'The politics of census: Fear of numbers and competing claims for representation in Naga society'. In: Arora, V. and Jayaram, N. (eds) *Democratisation in the Himalayas: Interests, conflicts, and negotiations*. New York: Routledge.

Eastern Mirror Nagaland (2017). 'Nagaland records highest rate of urban growth'. Dimapur. Available at: http://www.easternmirrornagaland.com/nagaland-records-highest-rate-of-urban-growth/ (accessed 14 July 2018).

Farrelly, N. (2009). '"AK47/M16 Rifle – Rs. 15,000 each": What price peace on the Indo-Burmese frontier?' *Contemporary South Asia* 17(3): 283–297. DOI: 10.1080/09584930903108960.

Fuller, N. (2001). 'The social constitution of gender identity among Peruvian men'. *Men and Masculinities* 3(3): 316–331. DOI: 10.1177/1097184X01003003006.

Gilbertson, A. (2014). 'A fine balance: Negotiating fashion and respectable femininity in middle-class Hyderabad, India'. *Modern Asian Studies* 48(1): 120–158. DOI: 10.1017/S0026749X1300019X.

Gill, P. (2005). 'Women in the time of conflict: The case of Nagaland'. *India International Centre Quarterly* 323(2): 213–226.

Government of India (1958). The Armed Forces (Assam and Manipur) Special Powers Act, 1958. 28.

Government of Nagaland (2015). Hornbill Festival. Available at: http://www.hornbillfestival.com/ (accessed 14 July 2015).

Government of Nagaland (2016b). Nagaland State Human Development Report 2016. Kohima.

Hausing, K.K.S. (2018). '"Equality of tradition" and women's reservation in Nagaland'. In: Wouters, J.J.P. and Tunyi, Z. (eds) *Democracy in Nagaland: Tribes, traditions, tensions*. Kohima: Highlander Books.

Hromadžic, A. (2015). *Citizens of an empty nation: Youth and state-making in postwar Bosnia-Herzegovina*. Philadelphia: University of Pennsylvania Press.

Imchen, T. (2017). 'Field notes: Women in the underground Nagaland freedom movement'. Humanities Across Borders. Available at: https://humanitiesacrossborders.wordpress.com/2017/11/07/field-notes-women-in-the-underground-nagaland-freedom-movement/.

Iralu, K.D. (2009). *The Naga saga*. 3rd ed. Kohima: Self Published.

Izzi, V. (2013). 'Just keeping them busy? Youth employment projects as a peacebuilding tool'. *International Development Planning Review* 35(2): 103–117. DOI: 10.3828/idpr.2013.8.

Kashypa, S.G. (2014). 'Nagaland police unearth illegal tax network run by NSCN(IM)'. New Delhi. Available at: http://indianexpress.com/article/cities/mumbai/nagaland-police-unearth-illegal-tax-network-run-by-nscnim/ Page (accessed 14 July 2019).

Kikon, D. (2017). 'Terrifying picnics, vernacular human rights, cosmos flowers: Ethnography about militarised cultures in Northeast India'. *Explorations: E-Journal of the Indian Sociological Society* 1(1).

Kolås, Å. (2017). 'Framing the tribal: Ethnic violence in Northeast India'. *Asian Ethnicity* 18(1): 22–37. DOI: 10.1080/14631369.2015.1062050.

Longchari, A. (2016). *Self determination: A resource for JustPeace.* Dimapur: Heritage Publishing House.

Lotha, A. (2009). *Articulating Naga nationalism.* New York: Thesis Submitted to Graduate Faculty in Anthropology, City University of New York.

Manchanda, R. and Kakran, S. (2017). 'Gendered power transformations in India's Northeast: Peace politics in Nagaland'. *Cultural Dynamics* 29(1): 63–82. DOI: 10.1177/0921374017709232.

Maringira, G. and Carrasco, L.N. (2015). '"Once a soldier, a soldier forever": Exiled Zimbabwean soldiers in South Africa'. *Medical Anthropology* 34: 319–335. DOI: 10.1080/01459740.2015.1038344.

Means, G.P. and Means, I.N. (1966). 'Nagaland – The agony of ending a guerrilla war'. *Pacific Affairs* 39(3): 290–313. DOI: 10.2307/2754274.

Messerschmidt, J.W. (2019). 'The salience of "hegemonic masculinity"'. *Men and Masculinities* 22(1): 85–91. DOI: 10.1177/1097184X18805555.

Mohaiemen, N. (2010). *Between ashes and hope: Chittagong Hill Tracts and the Blind Spot of Bangladesh nationalism.* Dhaka: Drishtipate Writers' Collective, Bangladesh.

Myrttinen, H. Khattab, L. and Naujoks, J. (2017). 'Re-thinking hegemonic masculinities in conflict-affected contexts'. *Critical Military Studies* 3(2): 103–119. DOI: 10.1080/23337486.2016.1262658.

Ní Aoláin, F., Cahn, N., and Haynes, D. (2016). 'Masculinities and child soldiers in post-conflict societies'. In: *Masculinities and the law: A multidimensional approach.* Minnesota: University of Minnesota Law School. DOI: 10.18574/nyu/9780814764039.003.0011.

Owen, J. (1844). *Notes on the Naga tribes in communication with Assam.* Calcutta: W.H Carey and Co.

Panwar, N. (2017). 'From nationalism to factionalism: Faultlines in the Naga insurgency'. *Small Wars and Insurgencies* 28(1): 233–258. DOI: 10.1080/09592318.2016.1233642.

Schwartz, S. (2010). *Youth and post-conflict reconstruction: Agents of change.* Washington D.C.: United States Institute of Peace.

Thong, T. (2010). '"Thy kingdom come": The impact of colonization and proselytization on religion among the Nagas'. *Journal of Asian and African Studies* 45(6): 595–609. DOI: 10.1177/0021909610373915.

Urdal, H. (2006). 'A clash of generations? Youth bulges and political violence'. *International Studies Quarterly* 50(3): 607–629.

Utas, M. (2012). 'Introduction : Bigmanity and network governance in African conflicts'. In: Utas, M. (ed.) *African conflicts and informal power: Big Men and networks*. London: Zed Books, 1–31.

Wilkinson, M. (2015). 'Negotiating with the Other: Centre-periphery perceptions, peacemaking policies and pervasive conflict in the Chittagong Hill Tracts, Bangladesh'. *International Review of Social Research Special Issue – Non State Armed Groups in National and International Politics* 5(2): 179–190.

Wollentz, G., Barišić, M., and Sammar, N. (2019). 'Youth activism and dignity in post-war Mostar – Envisioning a shared future through heritage'. *Space and Polity* 23(2): 197–215. DOI: 10.1080/13562576.2019.1635443.

Wouters, J.J.P. (2017). 'Who is a Naga village? The Naga "village republic" through the ages'. *The South Asianist* 5(1): 99–120.

Wouters, J.J.P. (2018). *In the shadows of Naga insurgency: Tribes, state, and violence in Northeast India*. New Delhi: Oxford University Press.

Part 2

Proximity

4   Nagaland Opening Up

Abstract

Chapter 4, 'Nagaland Opening Up', discusses the complex connections and networks in Nagaland that have emerged and changed since ceasefire, including accelerating economic ties to India alongside efforts to define and protect a distinct Naga identity. The state's opening up, in various forms, has encouraged new conflicts and contestations, over jobs and resources, representation, and over fears of demographic changes in Nagaland. Gender and men's traditional and often self-assumed roles as guardians of Naga territory, culture, and society are central in these conflicts and contestations.

Keywords: Liberalization, cosmopolitanism, marginalization, masculinity

Urbanization

The unofficial 'centre' of Dimapur is, arguably, City Tower. City Tower sits atop a roundabout at the corner of National Highway 129A and Circular Rd. To the east of the Tower are Asian Highway Road ('AH Road') and Eros Line, where the city's only two movie theatres sit within reach of several rifle and ammunition shops, Tibetan and Naga restaurants, and the Muslim cemetery. Further east is 5th, 6th, and 7th mile, three large suburbs extending to the edge of the town Chümoukedima, the last point of the foothills before the geography gets steeper and the 'highlands' that define the rest of the state begin. To the west of City Tower is Circular Rd, extending into Dimapur's suburbs, past the city's largest church – Dimapur Ao Baptist Church, and breaking off at the perpetually half-constructed Nagaland State Stadium. North of the Tower is Gollaghat Rd., a long flat highway extending into Assam, bounded by truck mechanics, tyre recyclers and courier offices, also a main route for alcohol being smuggled into Nagaland from Assam. To the south is Dimapur's central business district and Marwari Patti, a densely packed maze of streets and alleys and home to the city's largest market – 'Hongkong' Market. The central business district also houses a stretch of trader and importer offices and storage

Wilkinson, Matthew: *Borderland Anxieties. Shifting Understandings of Gender, Place and Identity at the India-Burma Border.* Amsterdam: Amsterdam University Press, 2023
DOI: 10.5117/9789463729789_CH04

shops adjacent to Dimapur's train station, several mosques and a Jain temple, and several more restaurants, poorly disguised liquor shops and bars. Budget hotels in the area cater to travelling businesspeople and people on short stays before moving to other parts of the state or taking a train outside the state. Essentially, all roads in Dimapur seem to, at some point, lead to City Tower.

While City Tower has often featured as a backdrop to dramatic events in the city, including several political rallies and a notorious lynching in 2015 (discussed in the following chapter), the tower itself is unassuming, a utilitarian design somewhat resembling a small Eiffel Tower with a digital clock at its top. Many town and city centres in Nagaland and in neighbouring states house similar towers, though often on a smaller scale. What is notable, however, are the changes taking place around City Tower in the central areas of Dimapur and the suburbs surrounding. In 2012, the central area surrounding the Tower, National Highway 29 heading towards the central business district as well as the streets coming off the highway were crowded with small two and three storey concrete shopfronts with large metal roller doors for security at entrances and rusted rebar rods exposed on rooftops. Some shops sold small farming equipment and two-stroke generators. Others sold clothing and textiles, most of which seemed to be marketed towards the local Marwari population – saris, kurtas, and men's shiny suits. Smaller local enterprises often had a family-run ambience and sometimes had clothes hanging on bamboo lines or strung between exposed rebar rods on the roof. Staff were often relatives of the owner and school-age children could occasionally be found standing in for the owner or for other workers. Open hours were often unpredictable and demeanours were relaxed and slow paced. Owners may close at any time of day to run errands, take rest, take lunch at home, or because business has been slow that day. Behind and above the shopfronts were small apartments and several low-cost dormitories typically catering to younger men travelling into and out of the state for work. Many buildings in the city centre were half-constructed, especially large parts of Hongkong Market, and rustic produce sellers, chai-wallahs and street kitchens had set up shop in the half-finished sections. Shop owners draped sheets or tarpaulins over missing walls or incomplete roofs to protect customers and equipment from the elements.

By 2020, these streets and alleys had changed dramatically. Over the last decade the city has experienced an urban boom involving the construction of new multi-storey shopping complexes, the expansion of residential areas, and higher-density residential complexes extending to the city's outer suburbs (Kikon and McDuie-Ra, 2021). Large shopping complexes and several office complexes now dominate parts of the central business district, many of which emerged from what were vacant lots in 2012. These newer buildings are typically made of reinforced cement concrete, glass and polished chrome and stand several storeys above the older buildings. The difference between the new commercial infrastructure and the older local businesses is dramatic. New commercial capital in the city embodies an image of modern development evoking high-rise construction, clean streets, and functional infrastructure that stands in stark contrast to the smaller shopfronts, potholed roads and dysfunctional infrastructure of the surrounding city (see Figure 3). New commercial developments sell a notably wider selection of goods and services than were available earlier, including international fashion brands, frozen foods, and small homewares. Other stores include mobile phone and computer stores, high-end electronics and whitegoods stores, dog-training services, car washing services, and travel agents offering international tourism packages, to list a few. These new developments appear to target an emerging market with tastes that reflect global consumer cultures. Trading hours in the state's urban centres have also expanded, a result of general perceptions that it is safer to travel around the city after dark, and serving a consumer base that have more disposable income to spend at bars and restaurants.[1] The older, smaller shops have not completely disappeared, and much of the central business area remains incomplete. Hongkong Market is still in a perpetual state of construction, and plastic tarpaulins still cover fruit sellers and smallgoods stalls on its ground floor. Extending past the central streets, though further and further away, small tea shops and eateries, mechanics, side-of-the-road butchers, and school supply shops continue to operate. Essentially, large changes are visible in the streets surrounding City Tower, changes to the face of the city itself, but also to consumption habits, ways of doing business, and what central Dimapur represents. This urbanization and market expansion is not limited to Nagaland's larger cities. In smaller towns and villages new construction projects are also taking place, though on a smaller scale. In Phek town, six hours east of Kohima, primarily made up of single-storey wooden houses with tin roofs, a new concrete shopping complex has been completed that brings with it the promise of consumer goods and conveniences on a scale that the town has not seen before. At four storeys tall, it is now the tallest building in the town, a claim that until 2018 was held by the Phek Town Baptist Church. Likewise, Mon town, the capital of Mon District in Nagaland's north, has experienced a dramatic growth in the past decade, with several high-priced hotels being constructed serving the district's influx of tourist groups and government workers attached to new development projects.

---

1 Several Dimapuri shop-owners made special note in 2017 that they can stay open for later now because more people are comfortable being in the street at later hours.

Figure 3 'Big Bazaar', Dimapur. 2019. Taken by author.

These new developments are telling of wider changes taking place in Nagaland as decades of armed conflict are being brought to a close through ceasefire. In the wake of ceasefire, doing business in the state has become safer and more predictable than it was during the 1970s, 1980s and 1990s. As the state becomes an easier place to do business, local incomes are growing, and a post-conflict economic 'boom' is taking place. Essentially, Nagaland is 'opening up' to new forms of investment, new flows of capital, goods, and services, and accelerated migration into the borderland. While there are many disruptions, fits and starts to the process and the state continues to be governed with security priorities, the changes are clear to see. New businesses are coming to the state and attempting to establish themselves in the emerging post-conflict economy. Goods and services that were previously less available across the state are much more available than ever before. Job advertisements for local businesses and for work in other parts of India are appearing at intersections, outside local colleges, and at other high-traffic areas. This is significant in a borderland state where, until very recently, conflict discouraged private investment except for a few extractive industries, which themselves were disrupted by nationalist groups, disagreements over land rights and ownership, and the state's poor infrastructure; that has historically been isolated from the outside world by protectionist policies; and has vehemently rejected its inclusion in India. In this chapter, I discuss the state's post-conflict 'opening up' and detail some of the ways the processes and dynamics of opening up manifest in Nagaland. These include new urban developments, in migration and out migration, and the state's growing tourism industry. Urbanization, migration and tourism are not an exhaustive list of changes that have taken place since ceasefire, and cannot offer a complete description of the complex flows between Nagaland and the outside world since ceasefire. However, these flows are important in Nagaland and are salient. They offer valuable insights into how life in Nagaland is changing in the wake of decades of armed conflict. I discuss the emergence of a post-conflict middle class in Nagaland, made possible by greater economic opportunities in the wake of conflict, and for whom India is more accessible and engaged in ways other than through experiences with Indian paramilitaries. Finally, I discuss how the process of opening up in the wake of ceasefire creates new forms of marginality in the state.

'Opening Up'

Throughout this book I employ the term 'opening up' to refer to liberalization taking place in Nagaland. 'Opening up' in Nagaland evokes liberalization in the sense that markets are expanding and new forms of capital are appearing; however, 'opening up' also evokes a more symbolic transformation involving new ways of interacting with, understanding, and imagining the Indian state, people and cultures from the plains, and other parts of the world outside of Nagaland. This transformation encompasses urbanization and the construction of new infrastructure, resource extraction and development (Kikon, 2019; Maaker et al., 2016), migration (Yadav and Shinde, 2015), and changing identities (Longkumer, 2018a). Some of these connections existed during Nagaland's conflict, although these were often of a much smaller and more localized scale (see von Fürer-Haimendorf, 1972). In the wake of ceasefire, larger scale and transformational investment is coming into Nagaland at an accelerating rate. As discussed in the previous chapter, Nagaland has been a resistant borderland state since India's 1947 independence. In 1951 a state-wide Naga plebiscite voted in support of complete secession from India. From 1956, the Naga National Council (NNC) led an armed resistance against India, which has evolved into an insurgent conflict that continues in parts of the state today. Essentially, Nagaland's inclusion as a part of India rested on militarization and exceptional laws used to enforce inclusion in the Indian union and curtail secessionist elements in the state (Means and Means, 1966). In the ceasefire era, however, Indian capital and closer ties to India are actively pursued alongside support for various forms of protected Naga autonomy. New commercial opportunities and investment flows bring jobs into a borderland state that hosts widespread unemployment and where there are few livelihood opportunities outside of agriculture or highly competitive jobs in the public sector.

These changes are difficult to show on paper. Record-keeping of population growth, urban growth, business and trade in Nagaland is poor at best and reliable figures that indicate Nagaland's economic, cultural, and political ties, as well as other changes taking place in the state are elusive. While Nagaland has recorded India's highest urban growth rate in the past two censuses (Eastern Mirror Nagaland, 2017), official statistics and figures for census and for elections in Nagaland since the 1970s have consistently been inaccurate or incomplete, and have often been doctored (Wouters, 2015). The 2001 census in Nagaland was marred by disagreements over borders, jurisdictions, and inflated numbers between tribes attempting to secure greater representation in political bodies and access to development funds based on population data (Das, 2017). The 2011 census was similarly contentious and reported population changes that were greatly divergent from earlier figures and local estimates (Agrawal and Kumar, 2013). Nagaland also hosts a large informal economy, which involves off-the-books sale of licit goods and services and a substantial trade in illicit goods such as drugs and alcohol, often through insurgent groups, military officers, and rumoured to involve corrupt government officials.[2] Migrants, often perceived to have come into the state illegally from Bangladesh, as well as a large population of Bihari and Bengali migrants, form an undocumented workforce that is difficult to count and assess, and adds to complications of rendering changes and the pace of change legible.

2   This was often brought up in conversations with anti-corruption activists in Nagaland between 2016 and 2020.

While difficult to empirically show, the evidence of Nagaland's post-conflict transformation is clear to see. Besides the obvious urban growth taking place, other changes in the state are occurring rapidly. Some restrictions on entry into the state have been relaxed and migration into Nagaland from other parts of India, and to a lesser degree from outside of India, is occurring at a growing rate. Out-migration is also accelerating, as Nagas leave the state to work, study, and live in other parts of India. This is not a new phenomenon, nor unique to Nagaland. For decades, Nagas have had to leave the state to access opportunities for education and work, usually to the nearby states of Assam and Meghalaya. However, in the wake of ceasefire, accelerating flows between India and Nagaland have encouraged even more movement into and out of Nagaland to more distant and larger cities in India such as New Delhi, Mumbai and Bangalore. Nagas and other Northeast Indians leave to study at universities and colleges that have better reputations and offer more courses than those in the Northeast, to work in a number of different fields, and to live in more connected and cosmopolitan cities (Karlsson and Kikon, 2017; McDuie-Ra, 2012b). While living in these larger Indian cities, Nagas and other Northeast Indian migrants do experience racism and discrimination, often due to their distinct appearance, different customs associated with diet such as eating beef and pork, and differences in social customs and norms between plains communities and highland tribal communities (McDuie-Ra, 2015). However, Naga and other Northeast Indian migrants also forge connections and friendships, build relationships and bonds, and form identities that are adjacent and overlapping (McDuie-Ra, 2016a). Migrant communities from Northeast India have established themselves outside of the state in hospitality and other service-oriented industries, often due to their English-language skills and distinct appearance (McDuie-Ra 2012c). Many come back to their communities and start training colleges and employment services to facilitate further migration (Karlsson and Kikon, 2017). Hence, out-migration from Northeast India, Nagaland included, since the late 1990s has encouraged a strengthening of connections with 'main' India, albeit alongside experiences of racism and discrimination. Nagaland's tourism industry has also emerged since ceasefire, marking a shift in the awareness of the state to the Indian public, and in the state's deliberate attempts to engage with Indian and international flows. The state's first tourism policy was passed in the year 2000 (Government of Nagaland, 2016b: 84). Also in 2000, Nagaland State Government inaugurated the Hornbill Festival at Kohima local ground with aims to revive, protect and preserve Naga heritage and to attract tourism (Government of Nagaland, 2015). While contentious, this also marks a significant part of the state's post-ceasefire opening up, encouraging a growing national and international awareness of Nagaland as a site for domestic and international tourists to visit (Longkumer, 2013; 2015). Overall, the easing of restrictions on entry and investment in the state, perceptions that ceasefire has leant a degree of stability to the state, and the emergence of a post-conflict economy – all related – encourage the further growth of interactions and connections between Nagaland and the outside world, especially India, thereby further accelerating the state's opening up.

Indian capital plays an immense role in these changes. Indian development funds are coming into the state with the goal of upgrading connective infrastructure and promoting 'peace-through-development' through greater regional engagement (Baruah, 2007: 17). Local investment also takes place, and locally owned enterprises have recently emerged and expanded. These are often smaller-scale developments, and either specialize in local handicrafts or are marketed towards a burgeoning tourism industry, adopting building styles that reflect a 'pan-Naga' tribal aesthetic – made with bamboo or local timber, with thatch roofing and featuring Naga head-hunter/warrior motifs and hornbill sculptures. Other investment from other parts of the world is also coming to the borderland, albeit much more recently and on a much smaller scale. Chinese department stores such as Miniso, and Japanese Usupso, both opened shops in Dimapur and Kohima in 2019, and Korean Gas Corp has made several attempts to establish a liquid-natural gas exporting unit in Nagaland since 2017. However, India's presence is much greater, much more visible, and takes place alongside Government-led efforts to bring Nagaland more closely into India's fold in an attempt to encourage peace-through-development (Baruah, 2009).

The expansion of Indian capital, goods, and services into Nagaland also taps into anxieties associated with Indian expansionism and the marginalization of Naga culture and society in Nagaland. India's commercial incursions into Nagaland have, predictably, been met with a degree of local anxiety and resistance, being seen as extensions, under the guise of commercial activities, of Hindu Indian norms and values (Longkumer, 2018c). However, these newer forms of India are, unlike earlier forms, not militarized and not associated with force and control. Indian investment and the growing presence of Indian consumer and investment spaces in the borderland make forms of development seem possible in ways that are hard to imagine happening otherwise. One discussant, David, offered his own perspective on India's more recent commercial and political involvement in Nagaland:

> Nagaland needs India to give us money. So much money comes in. What if they didn't? Look around, how much of these clothes are made in Nagaland? Nothing. Nothing we can make. How would people do? What? Will we all go back to the jungle? (laughs) All those big men who want independence, it's like [name removed] ... They talk about villages and traditions. They don't work, don't jhum [slash-and-burn agriculture] ... People in Dimapur, young people, we want to do business. We want it like Singapore. We can do business. Speak English. It's just the development, that's all. We can do call centres, selling jobs. It's better than the Indians can. It's just no development.[3]

This is especially the case in Nagaland's urban hubs, where more investment from the outside, most often India, enables new urban developments to be constructed at a very fast pace and new businesses to come to the state. New buildings such as modern shopping complexes are built using Indian capital and rented or owned by large corporations based in India. New shopping complexes such as S3 Shopping Mall, constructed in Dimapur 2017, Big Bazaar constructed in Dimapur in 2018, and S2 Shopping Mall, constructed in Kohima in 2018, are owned by Kolkata-based Tirupati Group, Mumbai-based Future Group and Kolkata based Tirupati Textrade Pty Ltd respectively. Indian mobile network providers such as Airtel and Jio cover most of Nagaland's urban centres and are extending their coverage into Nagaland's east. Indian car manufacturers such as TATA and Suzuki Maruti have opened new shopfronts in Dimapur and Kohima. Essentially, in the wake of ceasefire, India's presence in Nagaland is much more diverse and multifaceted. Indian paramilitaries are present and continue to be a source of insecurity in the state, albeit less so than before. Indian capital investment in Nagaland is increasingly the mode through which India is experienced and understood. As Nagas travel between Nagaland and India in growing numbers, young Nagas especially are working with and making friendships with non-Nagas (Angelova, 2015; Hazarika, 2018; McDuie-Ra, 2012b). This change occurs in tandem with the emergence of a post-conflict middle class who have new opportunities, greater mobilities, and hold de-territorialized aspirations where ideas of a 'good life' are less reliant on Naga independence and in

3   Interview (December 2017)

many ways are more dependent on closer economic, social and political ties outside of Nagaland.

Cosmopolitan Aspirations

Hannah and I sat in her kitchen discussing her business. She runs a small shop in central Kohima but leaves her two assistants in charge for much of the time the shop is open, while she travels back and forth between Delhi, Mumbai, and Bangalore. Before opening the shop, Hannah worked in Bangalore for a global IT corporation, earning a comfortable wage and enjoying many of the personal and social freedoms associated with living outside of the state. Three years ago, she left Bangalore to open the business in Kohima so that she could work her own hours and spend more time close to her family. The business is quiet most of the year but is busy during Nagaland's wedding season, between November and the end of December. Outside of those weeks, Hannah is free to visit friends in other parts of India and spend time with her family in Kohima. That Hannah spends long periods outside of Nagaland is nothing particularly new. While the state is changing, Nagaland continues to feel isolated and out-of-the-way for many, with poor infrastructure and relatively few opportunities for education, livelihoods, and leisure and recreation. Even in larger urban areas, roads are potholed and footpaths are muddy, and electricity and internet services are unreliable. People move outside of the state often, and have for decades. Nagas have moved to surrounding states such as Assam and Manipur for seasonal work for decades. Many communities live and work across India's border with Myanmar. During the heights of Nagaland's conflict, children were often sent to Meghalaya to receive a better education than was available in Nagaland at the time. What is new, however, is the freedom that Hannah can move to and from the state with, the distances moved, and the opportunities that come with increased mobility. This is a recent development. As Hannah described it in her own words:

> You need to understand, we are the first generation. My parents, they never could go to places like that [Bangalore, Mumbai, Delhi]. For us now, it's nothing, but for them, it's such a big deal, and that's for most of us here.[4]

Younger Nagas having vastly different opportunities to older generations, especially in the state's urban hubs, was an issue that reappeared across

4   Interview (December 2019)

multiple visits to the state between 2012 and 2020. Over conversations with friends in the state's larger towns, brief meetings with service workers such as hotel staff, and long discussions with journalists, shopkeepers, and local young business people, a common refrain that things were now more possible than they used to be was found, though what 'possible' means and the reasons for it were often unclear. Overall, ceasefire and liberalization have accelerated the conditions for the emergence of a post-conflict middle class whose experiences with India greatly differ from those of older Nagas, and for whom closer ties to India are more likely to be beneficial and in-demand, rather than oppressive and resisted. In other words, in the space of two generations, and in many cases just one, attitudes to and relationships with India have changed immensely, and young Nagas especially are cognizant of and involved in this change.

A middle class in Nagaland is not new. While many local and outside voices argue that Nagaland is an egalitarian and classless society (Lotha, 2009; Shimray, 2002), Nagaland has a well-established elite class that have maintained their status through dominating customary institutions and sections of the government (Sema, 2018). The nascent post-conflict middle class, however, is distinct from the elites that captured large sections of the state government and economy during Nagaland's decades of conflict. Groups such as the NNC derived a support base in a context where India was known almost exclusively through atrocities committed at the hands of Indian paramilitaries, especially during the years of initial militarization through the 1950s, 1960s and 1970s. From a population of Nagas living under this draconian occupation, a miniscule but influential tribal elite of Christian, Western educated Nagas emerged, many of whom had political connections and resources gathered through associations with Naga nationalist groups and through capturing sections of the conflict economy, while others had established themselves through accessing opportunities outside of these systems and outside of the state. This tribal elite was anchored to customary institutions and notions of reviving a loosely drawn traditional Naga society and defending a romanticized tribal way of life, marked by rigidly gendered customary institutions, utopian visions of Naga village democracies, and a social model of 'equality as tradition' espousing dogmatic gender roles and strict Christian moral sensibilities (Longkumer, 2018b). In the ceasefire era this imagined tribal utopia is open to challenge as many younger Nagas have a different relationship and different experiences with the Indian state. As Manchanda and Bose (2011: 55) argue, 'Phizo's imagined tribal utopia is threatened, especially after Naga statehood and the entry of the market economy. A small but "new" middle class comprising bureaucrats, businesspeople, lawyers, teachers, student unions and women's groups has emerged with consequences for reshaping Naga national aspirations'. While abductions, crossfire killings, rapes, and sexual abuse do continue to take place at the hands of Indian paramilitaries (McDuie-Ra, 2012c), the organized village and granary burning, summary executions, and systematic sexual abuse at the hands of Indian paramilitaries that took place in the earlier years of the conflict are far less prevalent today.

Nagaland's post-conflict middle class is distinct in terms of their urban location, education, qualifications, relative wealth, job opportunities, and cosmopolitan values. This small but growing social grouping navigates the traditional tribal institutions and patriarchal customs that aim to insulate and preserve a perceived natural order in the state, and modern socio-economic structures that challenge these institutions and norms through the disruptive potential of new economies and closer connection to the world outside the state. They move between Nagaland and other parts of India more regularly and benefit from closer relations with India in ways that older generations of Nagas did not. This is not an easy or a natural shift either, and involves demanding and highly competitive efforts by younger Nagas especially to be taught or to educate themselves to access new opportunities and take part in a more connected economy and culture (Kikon and Karlsson, 2020). This post-conflict middle class hold de-territorialized and cosmopolitan aspirations, delinked from pushes for Naga independence and informed by new possibilities brought through closer connections to India and new opportunities appearing at the post-conflict borderland. While this post-conflict middle class may support Naga autonomy and may sympathize with a wider push for Naga nationhood, they are also more attached to India, materially benefit from closer economic incorporation and greater political integration of Nagaland as a part of India and are more likely to see Indian identity and Naga identity as not being mutually exclusive. Hazarika (2017) sums up the generational nature of this change aptly, arguing that

> [a] new generation of younger people from the northeast [is] engaging with India and Indians, not as fighters against Delhi's Raj but as equals seeking acceptance of these rights and entitlements. Perhaps it is here that the core conditions of the region have changed—that a generation of young Indians from this area, exhausted by conflict and bloodshed, by ill will and stress, now seek to carve a new way for themselves based on the laws and systems of 'mainland' India. This is a remarkable change from an earlier time when their forebears, perhaps even their parents,

were involved in political and armed fights for independence or autonomy against India.

This emerging post-conflict social configuration has accrued the benefits of the Indian state structure and of market expansion into the borderland in ways that earlier tribal elites and older generations of Nagas have not. This post-conflict middle class engage more with the world outside of Nagaland through new mobilities and new technologies and live more urban and connected lifestyles that are entangled with Indian commerce, cultures and politics. They are more likely to engage with national and international ideas about governance and citizenship that are at odds with the tribal and clan-based patronage systems of governance in Nagaland, shaped through decades of conflict and state-dysfunction (Manchanda and Kakran, 2017: 65). Expanded markets and new goods and services available in the borderland, through greater access to Indian cities such as Delhi and Mumbai, make aspirations involving pan-global consumer cultures more realistic and possible. Urban lifestyles involving gainful employment and consumer options are more possible, offering livelihood options other than agriculture or highly competitive government jobs. Careerism, though still limited, is increasing in urban hubs where new commercial and investment spaces hire local workers and more capital is available to spend on consumer goods and services. Hence, this small but growing social grouping of educated and professional Naga men and women 'straddle both the traditional tribal institutions and modern socio-economic structures [and are] expanding the Naga public sphere and reshaping its society and politics' (Manchanda and Kakran, 2017: 64). These opportunities reflect the possibilities offered by expanding markets in Nagaland in the wake of conflict and a greater ability to travel outside of Nagaland, shared by everyone, including Hannah in the example above.

Through these mobilities and through interacting with new capital in the borderland, members of this nascent middle class are exposed to national and international ideas and developments about citizenship, agency, and gender that are very much at odds with older norms and sensibilities (Manchanda and Bose, 2011: 55). New opportunities for Naga women that were much less available in the years before ceasefire have appeared, including the opportunity to travel to other parts of India for work, to start a business at home in the borderland, and to invest time and effort into careers with the potential for promotions and upward mobility. In many senses, women in Nagaland have been especially able to reap the benefits of the state's post-conflict economic expansion, often having more positive experiences when working and studying in larger Indian cities and accessing opportunities for higher education that many men in the state appear to forego (Shankar Das, 2019; McDuie-Ra, 2012b). These opportunities have the potential to challenge conflict-informed ideas about gender and the rigidly gendered structure of Naga society in ways that were not challenged before, in particular ideas that women are unable to participate in politics in Naga society, and men hold a 'natural strength' that is inclined towards protecting, representing, and leading Naga society.

State Stadium, Dimapur

It was approaching midday in Dimapur. I had been visiting the city's incomplete State Stadium over the past two weeks, coming at different times of day, taking note of who spends time there, what they do, and where possible sitting and talking to locals about their use of the space and what led them to the stadium. State Stadium is a part of Dimapur that a wide variety of people congregate at during the day, and at night has a reputation as a magnet for drinking, drug use, prostitution, graffiti and salacious activities. The site, previously known as Lalmatee, has a chequered history. In the 1980s and 1990s Lalmatee was a dumping ground for the bodies of suspected spies, drug dealers and drug addicts executed by Naga nationalist groups. One discussant mentioned that for a period in the early 1990s, a body was found at the site every other week. From the mid-1990s, the Nagaland State Government has attempted to remake the site and amend its seedy reputation. These efforts involved turning the large vacant lot into a multi-sports complex, complete with a colosseum-type stadium, athlete accommodation, indoor badminton courts and an indoor gymnasium. However, construction was left incomplete amid speculations of embezzlement and graft which were especially rife in the early 2000s. Various attempts have been made to resume construction, although so far these have been delayed, resumed, and delayed again as funds are either suspended by Nagaland State Government or embezzled by construction contractors. Ironically, the half-constructed efforts to cleanse State Stadium of its reputation for crime, moral corruption and vice have themselves become landmarks to embezzlement, financial corruption and state dysfunction.

Despite the presence of some unsavoury elements, State Stadium is an important part of Dimapur. The city has grown rapidly since the early 2000s. However, with the exception of some vacant lots near the railway tracks and an abandoned Assam Rifles camp near Zeliangrong Village in the city's south, there are very few open public spaces in the growing city. The city centre is crowded and loud. People spending time in a shop or outside of a shop in the city centre for long periods without good reason are looked upon with suspicion and are quickly moved on by shopkeepers or security guards. The city's surrounding suburbs are made up of close-knit communities who are often from the same tribe. Neighbours notice, are suspicious of, and talk about any new visitors or sordid activities in their neighbourhoods. State Stadium, on the other hand, is open, does not have security guards, and is interspersed with concrete ruins and overgrown bushes that offer relative privacy. People can spend time at State Stadium without standing out or drawing attention. The site is located close to the city centre, but is relatively quiet and has little traffic, except for teenagers occasionally learning to drive in and around the site's dirt-topped parking lot. Because of its location, openness, and the lack of alternative sites in the city, State Stadium has come to fulfil a number of important roles for various groups. In the early mornings, local residents jog its perimeter and a Zumba dance class is held on the grassy field at the front of the stadium. In the afternoon and at night, teenagers bring their love interests to the stadium to evade prying relatives and gossipy neighbours, and college students smoke, drink, and loiter around the parking lot near the entrance. In the hours in-between morning and evening, the stadium hosts a rabble of cows and goats owned by Bihari herders and a regular rotation of older men who come to the site to drink, use drugs, and socialize away from home. These men are not homeless, but have few other alternative places to congregate.

I had stopped at the Stadium's parking lot, a dirt patch surrounded by large, shady trees, to take shelter from the sun. It was approaching 35 degrees Celsius, and humid. Nearby, three middle-aged men were sitting under an Amilisu tree. The younger of the three was leaning over a folded newspaper, mixing loose tobacco with cannabis. One of the men was smoking a homemade bong fashioned from a plastic Mirinda (orange soft drink) bottle and a Kingfisher beer can. The eldest looking of the group was watering down Old Monk rum, the cheapest available in the state, in a plastic glass while gesturing at the graffiti scrawled on the wall across from us, a cartoon of a naked woman with her legs spread. I made small talk with the men, mentioning the heat, asking what they do for a living, whether they are married or not, and how often they come to the stadium. One of the men was married and employed in a government job in a town several hours north of Dimapur. We joked about the travelling time between Dimapur and his work posting, as he clearly implied that he rarely attends work. The other two men were unmarried and not working. I asked them what they do with the free time. One of the men raised both arms in the air and loudly exclaimed, 'Timepass, what else to do?'

The circumstances of the men at State Stadium reflected those of many other men I had encountered in Nagaland of similar ages. These men could be easily found in disused peri-urban sites like the Stadium, in dark taverns serving cheap and often adulterated liquor, and in cheap local hotels dotted throughout the state. Although not all were unemployed, these men appeared to experience long periods of idle time, were somewhat disconnected from Nagaland's recent economic expansion, and spent much of their time drinking, using cheap and easily sourced drugs, and sleeping. During months of fieldwork, it became clear that a significant number of households in Nagaland host at least one man in a similar situation – often being long-term unemployed and with substance abuse problems. While Nagaland has a high unemployment rate (Kikhi, 2006), and drug and alcohol abuse is common (Kermode et al., 2007, 2009), these men appeared to constitute a distinct population who are recognized as problematic, unemployed or underemployed, and prone to substance problems. These men were sometimes referred to as Nagaland's 'lost generation', a term that surfaced repeatedly in discussions in Nagaland between 2016 and 2020, often without prompting. This 'lost generation' appears to have been relegated to new margins at the changing frontier. They are too old, they have few in-demand skills, and do not conform to the cosmopolitan norms emerging in the changing borderland state and in larger cities in other parts of India. The men being referred to were of similar ages, between 40 and 50 years old. It is important to note that this 'lost generation' by no means constitutes all men in this age group in Nagaland. Indeed, the men that this chapter is concerned with constitute a minority, albeit a sizeable minority, of men from this age group. There is a much larger population of men in Nagaland who have gainful employment, are active in the church and community, live up to their roles in the community, and have adjusted well to life since the closing of conflict and the emergence of new opportunities in the state. However, the emergence of Nagaland's 'lost generation' in the years following ceasefire and during the state's opening up suggests that liberalization creates new margins that often assumedly empowered groups, such as men of 'middle-adulthood' living in a patriarchal society, find themselves in. Essentially, in the wake of ceasefire and liberalization, changes are taking place that are marginalizing in ways that often challenge established ideas of patriarchy, status, and masculinity.

Timepass Ase

It was 11:30am. Simon and I were sitting in an eatery in Dimapur, sharing a plate of fried pork and dried chillies. This was a welcome back meal. I had known Simon for several years, and it had been a long time since we had last spoken. I asked about what Simon was doing with himself and what I had missed since my last visit. Simon once worked in a large Indian city, and says he was successful there. But since returning to Nagaland nearly fifteen years ago he has not been able to find a job, has gotten by with little to no income, and has lived with his elderly father. In these years, some of Simon's peers had left the state, and others have found secure work in Nagaland's public service, while Simon has stayed at home and attempted various money-making projects including a restaurant, a travelling band, and a food delivery service. The last time we spoke, he was attempting to convert his father's house into a bed-and-breakfast to rent out to tourists. It seems that project had been postponed. The bed-and-breakfast had sat unfinished for years now as a concrete skeleton and piles of rusted metal and rotting bamboo on his father's roof. Now, Simon was considering a new business, a food cart. He was nervous about it. Simon's failed attempts to pull together an income have left him somewhat despairing, and it is apparent that with each new project, a pessimism has crept in. Each venture seems less realistic, and the efforts taken to pursue each business venture seem more lack-lustre. The risk of business failure, or more accurately, business fizzling-out, is compounded and self-fulfilled by Simon's habit of drinking throughout the day and his difficulties maintaining regular hours. Other discussants had also occasionally mentioned these failed projects, humorously saying that if Simon is involved in a business, they want nothing to do with it.

As the last morsels of smoked pork disappeared from our plates, Simon looked up at me with a grin. 'Peg?' he asked. By 'peg', Simon meant a shot of cheap rum or whisky, popular in Nagaland because of its potent alcohol content, relative availability despite Nagaland's alcohol ban, and low price. Simon, and men like Simon, are some of its largest consumers. I paid our bill and we walked across the main street and down a slim alleyway. An unassuming shop populated by a table and lined with water bottles is our first stop. Otherwise empty shops with a conspicuous number of water bottles on display is often a sign that alcohol is available there or close by. Simon talked to the two boys at the table, and one ducked behind the shop and returned with a black plastic bag. Inside the bag was a bottle of Old Monk rum and two plastic cups. Simon turned to me to pay for the liquor.

We flagged an auto down and went to the site of Simon's prospective business venture, a lawn behind a row of shops on the outskirts of Dimapur. Simon twisted the bottle open and poured a generous peg into each plastic cup. As Simon discussed the big plan, to wheel the food cart to local fairs and festivals, there was an optimism in his voice. However, it was already January, the end of the festival and holiday season, so most of the big events in Dimapur had already been held. I attempted to change the topic, rather than raise questions about the new business venture. I told Simon about the men I met earlier at the stadium, about how I had noticed a lot of older men in the state in similar positions. I asked Simon why so many men spent so much time passing time, or 'time-passing' in Nagaland with drugs and alcohol. Simon's response brought together his own recognition that it is a generational activity, and that it involves alcohol, limited options, and a sense of security rooted in men's rights to inherit ancestral property:

> Us Naga guys, you know why we time-pass, [not] because we're lazy, it's because we have the property, we're the bosses, even for a jobless man, he's the boss in his house. All of these men staying at home, they get their food cooked, they get some money for booze, and they have the house and the land to own. What extra can you get from working then? Especially here. Do you think I'm going to go and work in a shop? Selling jeans? Imagine a Naga man doing this things. We just don't have that culture, can't tell us what to do. As long as we have the land though, whatever happens we're OK ... All these men, all the drinking, jobless, but whatever happens I have land, we have land, a house, it's security. Why would you work? If you knew you'd be OK? Here, you wouldn't.[5]

Simon and I continued to discuss his future business plans. The bottle of Old Monk was emptied over the next hour. Simon lit a Gold-Flake cigarette while I asked him what he was doing with the rest of the day. Mimicking a hand grenade, Simon took the empty bottle of Old Monk and threw it across the lawn while exhaling loudly and exclaiming, 'I don't know bro, timepass ase?'.[6] The bottle landed next to a pile of about a half dozen other empty Old Monk bottles.

5   Interview (October 2019)
6   In Nagamese, depending on its inflection 'ase' (pronounced ah-sey) is often used as a question or an exclamation at the end of a sentence.

Small Stain on Your Tooth

Thomas was in his late forties and divided his time between living with his wife and children and living with his mother in one of Nagaland's larger urban areas. He is college-educated with a bachelor's degree and has worked for Nagaland State Government in the past. He has told me he works in a government job, and that his position is very important, involving regular meetings with high-level bureaucrats, being driven in a new Bolero four-wheel-drive, and regularly taking helicopter rides between villages. His family has told me none of this is true, and that he has been jobless for the last decade. Thomas' family have informed me that they do not think he has any intention of getting a job and that they are perplexed as to why he is at peace living off his mother while only sometimes staying with his wife and children. Discussions with those close to Thomas revealed their own frustration and confusion with his scenario. One of Thomas's family members rhetorically asked, 'Why does he come and stay here? He has a home, his wife is waiting for him … no job, no nothing, I don't know what he's doing here all the time'.[7] Through several discussions over a period of months it became clear that Thomas is also very agitated with his situation, but also come to terms with what he refers to as his 'plot in life'. As Thomas describes it, he has worked before, and is now spending time on various projects. These projects were not given further detail and when asked to elaborate, Thomas changed the topic quickly.

While living with his mother, Thomas drinks throughout the day. He usually drinks Officer's Choice scotch alone in his bedroom. One wall of the bedroom is lined with empty bottles of Officer's Choice. Thomas spends most of his days watching daytime Hindi soap operas and listening to 1980s American 'hair-metal' bands including Poison and Warrant. He is often eager to run errands for people in the house, and whether sober or intoxicated regularly climbs into his car, a rusted Maruti hatchback that needs a few attempts before it starts, to buy milk powder, soap, or other small groceries from local shops. Thomas often becomes violent when very intoxicated. Several family members and neighbours have had tense confrontations with him about how loud he plays his music and about his habit of wandering the surrounding streets late at night. When asked about fights in his home, Thomas says that they have 'disrespected me, I do my life, they need to do theirs'.

7   Interview (January 2018)

I had spent the morning walking with Thomas in his neighbourhood as he pointed out some of the places that were once used by Naga insurgent groups and sites where the military once kept large gun emplacements. Later in the day, I needed to go to Dimapur's city centre to buy groceries and new notepads. To break the silence while we walked, I asked Thomas where I could get decent writing pads. Thomas listed some of the smaller shops around Church Rd, in Dimapur's centre. He then mentioned that I could probably find better quality paper at Big Bazaar, but that he wouldn't come with me. As we walked back to his mother's house, Thomas talked about Big Bazaar and other new shops opening up in Dimapur. He made a special point that new shopping complexes, bars, and restaurants in the city are for 'those rich folks, not for guys like me'. At one-point Thomas exclaimed, 'All of these bars, fancy restaurant, Big Bazaar, how many normal folks are in [these places]? It's just for the rich … can't dress like church, small stain on your tooth, you're outside'. Thomas then told the story of his own experience with Big Bazaar.

Big Bazaar is one of the largest and newest shopping complexes in Dimapur. I had watched the complex itself being constructed between 2016 and 2018, with the construction process stopping and then restarting several times over this period. Big Bazaar sells various Indian-made mass-produced clothes, kitchen goods, children's toys and also frozen foods and ready-made meals. The Big Bazaar chain of supermarkets is one of India's largest, and most large Indian cities, even in Northeast India, have one Big Bazaar in them. When Big Bazaar opened, it was an event for the city, celebrated as bringing new products and jobs to Dimapur, and implicitly viewed as a sign that Dimapur was coming up and stood on par with other cities that had their own Big Bazaar. The monolithic building itself has a clean façade with a large billboard advertising some of its products on its street-facing wall. Two security guards are posted at the entrance, checking bags of those entering the store, walking people through metal detectors at the front doors, and checking bags of those leaving the store. Thomas attempted to buy goods from Big Bazaar before but was turned back at this point. The security guards at the entrance approached Thomas as he was entering, asked Thomas whether he had been drinking, which he had, and told him he cannot come in if he has taken alcohol. Security then escorted Thomas down the stairs in the front of the complex and sternly advised him to move away from the building while people in the store and in the street watched and stared. While Big Bazaar does not have an explicit dress code, Thomas is adamant that his appearance was key to being denied entry to the shopping complex. Thomas believed the alcohol policy was an excuse to deny him entry, and that the guards did not want him there because he does not, in his own words, 'dress like church', and that he looks too casual for the store.

Thomas' experience was telling of some of the more banal ways exclusion takes place in the liberalizing borderland. While he has failed to find work and spends significant lengths of time drinking and running neighbourhood errands, Thomas has also experienced marginalization and being left out of the emerging post-conflict economy in Nagaland in a literal sense. New commercial spaces, such as Big Bazaar and other shopping complexes in Nagaland's growing urban hubs are not explicitly exclusive. However, these spaces are marketed towards a consumer class with disposable incomes who embody the sensibilities and etiquette of a vaguely drawn but widely understood pan-global cosmopolitan citizen. This is especially the case with the customs surrounding alcohol and drug consumption, standards of dress, and standards of personal hygiene, which Thomas refers to as 'small stain on your tooth'. In other words, liberalization in the borderland, as experienced by Thomas, involves being denied access to new consumer spaces based on his appearance, standards of dress, and likely, his alcohol consumption habits.

New Marginalities in the Liberalizing Borderland

Liberalization is a phenomenon marked by the rapid expansion of consumer cultures, the emergence of a consumption-focused middle class who have disposable incomes, and the increasing availability of a variety of commodities in the market targeted towards this consumption-focused middle class (Mathur, 2010). Liberalization has far-reaching social and cultural effects, extending beyond the availability of goods and services and new livelihood opportunities, to shape identities, relationships, and cultures according to market-focused norms and values (Zabiliute, 2016). Liberalization encourages the emergence of middle-class norms and sensibilities defined by a cosmopolitan consumerism, where '[consumer] commodities are seen as positive social identifiers, and where visible, aspirational consumption has become a key signifier of middle class status' (Nielsen and Wilhite, 2015: 383). The consumer middle class can be accessed and middle-class status achieved through consumption and through navigating the new economic landscape to scale old social and cultural barriers (Osella and Osella, 1999). This is done through buying the right clothes (Gilbertson, 2014), through owning cars (Nielsen and Wilhite, 2015), through eating Western diets and adopting Western eating customs such as cutlery and disposable food packaging (Aloia et al., 2013), through collecting qualifications and degrees from various legitimate and illegitimate institutions (Fernandes, 2006: 92), and through engaging with and immersing themselves in cosmopolitan sites such as large shopping malls and showrooms (Zabiliute, 2016).

Liberalization gives rise to new social divisions, new forms of marginalization, and new assertions and contestations that are linked to the ways that this typically younger urban middle class have been able to capture the benefits of liberalization. Marginality in this sense involves a limited ability to engage with the changing context that surrounds one's life. This new marginality is embedded in processes of liberalization and the changes associated with the rapid expansion of markets, urban spaces, and technologies associated with liberalization. Zabiliute (2016: 271), when describing these changes, argues that 'new urban spaces are oriented towards a consuming public, and everyone who falls outside of this category is excluded, as cities become gradually enclosed along the lines of class and caste'. This exclusion is not only limited to urban spaces, but also takes place in rural areas where, for example, traditional and communal land is being converted to individual lots and where agriculture is being oriented towards a global market, and those who cannot adapt to these changes are in many senses left behind (Maaker et al., 2016). Di Nunzio (2019: 2) offers an insight into this form of marginality through the experiences of two men, Haile, aged 49, and Ibrahim, aged 39, in Addis Ababa:

> As their country seemed to flourish and high-rise steel-and-glass buildings began popping up in Addis Ababa's wealthier neighbourhoods ... Haile's and Ibrahim's condition of marginality persisted. For them and many of their peers in inner city Addis, marginality was no longer an experience of a widely shared condition of scarcity but a sense of being out of tune with history.

As cities and frontiers globalize and liberalize, urban spaces especially become even more oriented towards consumer consumption and the cultures that surround consumption. Being able to buy new goods, especially new technologies such as mobile phones and to pay for internet access is increasingly important. Meeting sites and spaces of leisure and recreation increasingly take place in consumer spaces such as shopping complexes, cinemas, restaurants, and cafes. Cosmopolitan fashions are often marketed towards younger demographics, standards of dress are linked to an ambiguously global urban style that is legitimated by its association with consumer cultures and is difficult to emulate locally. Men without work are less able to engage with consumer cultures as workers and as consumers, and through this inability, are often relegated to a growing liberalization underclass (Zabiliute, 2016: 271). The close links between masculinity and employment have been discussed in myriad ethnographies of men (Elmhirst, 2007; Fuller, 2001; Guttman, 1996; Walter et al., 2004). The ability to find and maintain employment is, almost universally, a fundamental aspect of masculinity. While in many contexts women may do more work, men's work is afforded a higher status and a central place in men's identities (Connell, 2005: 78). Reflecting on the earlier research by Gilmore (1991), Connell (2005: 32) postulated that 'the cultural function of masculine identity is to motivate men to work'. However, structural changes in the global economy have led to greater participation by women in paid work, and simultaneously to increasing rates of under-and un-employment among men. This has severely undermined and displaced many men's identities as providers and, on a larger scale, as the turning cogs at the centre of a patriarchal economy and society (Cleaver, 2002). Being unable to work does not only mean being unable to satisfy masculine norms of having employment and bringing resources into the home.

India's post-1991 liberalization is typically discussed as a transition from socialist-style development embodied in monolithic public infrastructure projects such as dams, highways, factory-cities, and massive agricultural projects to export oriented commodity markets, imported consumer goods, and competitive labour markets (Das et al., 2021; Lahiri, 2010; Ramakrishnan, 2014). As Fernandes (2006: 37) argues, 'if the tenets of Nehruvian development could be captured by symbols of dams and factories, the markers of Rajiv Gandhi's regime shifted to commodities that would tap into the tastes and consumption practices of the urban middle class'. For many communities in India's borderlands, however, the kind of monolithic state-led development described above is lacking and has been since Independence. Large sections of the Northeast and other borderlands such as Jammu and Kashmir have, until recently, been relatively untouched by the Nehruvian style of development that marked much of post-independence India. Rather, development in these areas follows securitized priorities, where state resources and state-led development projects serve the needs of a hyper-modern military and support the logistics of enforcing state-authority onto resistant populations. In these areas, liberalization and economic opportunities are presented, and delivered, alongside continuing military occupation, exceptional laws, and state-led violence. McDuie-Ra (2012a: 40) argues, with reference to the wider Northeast region, that 'the mistrust of the past and present lingers, but is assuaged by a mixture of necessity and opportunity'. In this sense, liberalization in the borderland encourages complex relationships between borderland communities and the central state, where resentment and distrust exist alongside new opportunity and connection. At the post-conflict borderland, a rapid 'opening up' of these territories to new investments and to new markets has the effect of magnifying the inclusive and exclusive aspects of liberalization. McDuie-Ra discusses some of the ways a similar dynamic of opening up in the city of Imphal, in Manipur, involves various forms of inclusion and exclusion, where Imphal's liberalization and the transition of the city from a militarized frontier city to a crucial piece of India's gateway to Southeast Asia involves selective forms of resistance and engagement (McDuie-Ra, 2016b).

The ways liberalization takes place in Nagaland creates new opportunities for some groups and marginalizes others, often in ways that challenge understandings of politics, gender and empowerment in borderlands. The borderland is being redefined and reoriented from a space marked by isolation, conflict, and especially few livelihood options towards a more connected and commercially engaged site with new mobilities and a wider selection of livelihood opportunities. This change is also especially gendered, presenting Naga women in particular with opportunities to be more mobile, become more economically empowered, and gain new forms of independence that challenge a conflict-informed patriarchal social and political structure in the state that assumes the survival of Naga society depends on the maintenance of a rigidly gendered social and political order. As paid work becomes more common a widening gap has emerged between Nagas who are able to access and engage with the expanding market economy, and Nagas who cannot. For those who are less able to take part in the expanding working economy in the state or who are unable to work in other Indian cities, this gap is marked. It is marked in cultural differences between those who are more engaged with Indian and global markets and hence more engaged with Indian and global consumer cultures. It is also marked by how people spend their time and where they spend their time. For example, new shopping complexes and the higher-end bars, restaurants and coffee shops that have appeared in Nagaland's urban areas are directed towards an emerging consumer class who have disposable incomes and consumer tastes that reflect a pan-Indian cosmopolitan urban lifestyle. Older men in particular are less able to engage with and be included in this cosmopolitan culture, and thus, are relegated to its margins. Thomas's references to not dressing 'like church' and to stained teeth were allusions to this emerging class divide in the frontier. Being less able to take part in Nagaland's new economy, older men in Nagaland are, in many senses, being excluded, not only from new urban spaces, but from the cultures associated with these spaces. Emerging forms of marginalization experienced by groups of men in Nagaland in the ceasefire era are also compounded by understandings of Naga society as patriarchal and as inherently structured for the empowerment of Naga men. In many senses these understandings of Naga society are accurate. Nagaland is a patriarchy – men possess rights to hold political positions and own ancestral property that women do not. However, as Nagaland opens up, the appearance of new commercial infrastructure, new markets, and new forms of mobility in the frontier are empowering, for younger Nagas especially, but also exclusionary, for older Nagas and many older Naga men in particular. Marginality is hidden and exists alongside patriarchal customary institutions and cultural norms of men being 'heads of the household' and authorities in public and private matters.

Conclusion

Since ceasefire, new Indian capital and non-militarized forms of the Indian state are appearing in the borderland at an accelerating rate. New investors are building modern shopping and office complexes, opening businesses that sell goods and services that were previously unavailable, and providing jobs in a state with high unemployment and few opportunities for work outside of the public sector. This process is uneven, and occurs alongside ongoing militarization, non-state armed groups, and continuing state dysfunction, but it is ongoing and accelerating, nonetheless. This process is also difficult to document, but is visible to see in the form of new commercial infrastructure appearing throughout the state, especially in Nagaland's larger urban centres. Businesses and trading hours are expanding, new consumer spaces are emerging, and markets are selling goods and services that were not available before. India is attached to almost all of these changes. Indian private investment funds and owns much of the new commercial infrastructure, alongside ongoing efforts by the Indian state to bring Nagaland and the wider Northeast Indian region closer into the Indian fold. Indian-led capital investment in the borderland especially makes ideas of modern development and functional infrastructure more possible and has given rise to a post-conflict middle class for whom India is less associated with draconian violence and military occupation, and more associated with job creation, opportunity, and mobility. While India's presence in Nagaland is still marked by military occupation and an ongoing state of exception, India is also increasingly associated with new forms of development, new commercial spaces, and new goods and services in the borderland. Opening up fosters the emergence of a post-conflict Naga middle class who are more urban, have more options in terms of employment and livelihoods, and travel between India and Nagaland more often. Younger Nagas have especially benefitted from the changes taking place in the state since ceasefire. Their mobility, English speaking skills, and Western cosmopolitan dispositions are in high demand by Indian corporations based in larger Indian cities, and also by corporations expanding into the borderland. In particular, the aspirations of this middle class are de-linked from pushes for independence and detached from the visions for independent village democracies imagined by Naga nationalist groups. Rather, aspirations among this post-conflict middle class are more closely linked to consumer cultures and individual notions of success through career opportunities and new mobilities, made more possible by Indian capital coming into Nagaland. This is a significant shift for a borderland society that is emerging from decades of conflict that was aimed at resisting and repelling the Indian state and Indian influences. However, opening up and liberalization is a process that also involves exclusion and marginalization. With the emergence of a more open economy that contributes towards and caters to an emerging consumer economy, and the emergence of a middle class that can take part in this economy, new divergences are also taking form. For a population of older men in the state especially, Nagaland's post-conflict changes are witnessed from the sidelines. The emergence of a more connected and youth-oriented post-conflict economy relegate these older and lesser skilled men to the margins of the post-conflict economy and society. The ability to find work is not the exclusive tenet of masculinity in Nagaland. As I discuss in the following chapter, masculinity and men's roles in Naga society are enmeshed in a nexus of customary titles and decision-making roles, land-ownership, and authority in the household, along with the ability to work and provide for the household. As Nagaland's economy changes and as life in the state is more entangled with Indian and overseas markets work has become more central, and other tenets of masculinity, arguably, more tenuous.

References

Agrawal, A. and Kumar, V. (2013). 'Nagaland's demographic somersault'. *Economic & Political Weekly* 48(39): 69–74.

Aloia, C.R. Gasevic, D. Yusuf, S. et al. (2013). 'Differences in perceptions and fast food eating behaviours between Indians living in high- and low-income neighbourhoods of Chandigarh, India'. *Nutrition Journal* 12(1). DOI: 10.1186/1475-2891-12-4.

Angelova, I. (2015). 'Building a "home" away from home: The experiences of Young Naga Migrants in Delhi'. *Journal of the Anthropological Society of Oxford* 7(2): 153–167.

Baruah, S. (2007). *Durable disorder: Understanding the politics of Northeast India*. New Delhi: Oxford University Press. DOI: 10.1093/acprof:oso/9780195690828.001.0001.

Baruah, S. (2009). *Beyond counter-insurgency: Breaking the impasse in Northeast India*. Oxford: Oxford University Press.

Cleaver, F. (2002). 'Men and masculinities: New directions in gender and development'. In: Cleaver, F. (ed.) *Masculinities Matter! Men, Gender and Development*. London: Zed Books.

Das, D.K. Erumban, A.A. and Mallick, J. (2021). 'Economic growth in India during 1950–2015: Nehruvian socialism to market capitalism'. In: *Journal of Economic Surveys*, 1 July 2021, 926–951. Blackwell Publishing Ltd. DOI: 10.1111/joes.12350.

Di Nunzio, M. (2019). *The act of living: Street life, marginality, and development in urban Ethiopia*. Cornell: Cornell University Press.

Elmhirst, R.J. (2007). 'Tigers and gangsters: Masculinities and feminised migration in Indonesia'. In: Smith, D.P and Stockdale, A. (eds) *Population, space and place*. New York: John Wiley & Sons, Ltd. DOI: 10.1002/psp.435.

Fernandes, L. (2006). *India's new middle class: Democratic politics in an era of economic reform*. Minneapolis: University of Minnesota Press. DOI: 10.4324/9780203814116.

Gilmore, D. (1991). *Manhood in the making: Cultural concepts of masculinity*. New Haven: Yale University Press.

Hazarika, S. (2017). 'Why the young from India's northeast are building bridges with the country's big cities'. *Quartz*, 25 December.

Hazarika, S. (2018). *Strangers no more: New narratives from India's northeast*. New Delhi: Aleph Book Company.

Karlsson, B.G. and Kikon, D. (2017). 'Wayfinding: Indigenous migrants in the service sector of metropolitan India'. *South Asia: Journal of South Asia Studies* 40(3). Routledge: 447–462. DOI: 10.1080/00856401.2017.1319145.

Kermode, M., Longleng, V., Singh, B.C., et al. (2007). 'My first time: Initiation into injecting drug use in Manipur and Nagaland, North-East India'. *Harm Reduction Journal* 4(19). DOI: 10.1186/1477-7517-4-19.

Kermode, M., Longleng, V., Singh, B.C., et al. (2009). 'Killing time with enjoyment: A qualitative study of initiation into injecting drug use in North-East India'. *Substance Use & Misuse* 44(8): 1070–1089. DOI: 10.1080/10826080802486301.

Khutso, R. (2018). 'Shifting democratic experiences of Nagas'. In: Wouters, J.P. (ed.) *Democracy in Nagaland: Tribes, traditions, tensions*. Kohima: Highlander Books.

Kikhi, K. (2006). *Educated unemployed youth in Nagaland: A sociological study.* New Delhi: Akansha Publishing House.

Kikon, D. and Karlsson, B.G. (2020). 'Light skin and soft skills: Training indigenous migrants for the hospitality sector in India'. *Ethnos* 85(2): 258–275. DOI: 10.1080/00141844.2018.1543717.

Lahiri, S. (2010). 'At home in the city, at home in the world: Cosmopolitanism and urban belonging in Kolkata'. *Contemporary South Asia* 18(2): 191–204. DOI: 10.1080/09584935.2010.481726.

Longkumer, A. (2013). 'Who sings for the Hornbill?: The performance and politics of culture in Nagaland, Northeast India – Part I'. *The South Asianist Blog* Available at: https://thesouthasianist.wordpress.com/2013/02/14/who-sings-for-the-hornbill-the-performance-and-politics-of-culture-in-nagaland-northeast-india-part-i/.

Longkumer, A. (2015). '"As our ancestors once lived": Representation, performance, and constructing a national culture amongst the Nagas of India'. *Himalaya, the Journal of the Association for Nepal and Himalayan Studies* 35(1): 51–64.

Longkumer, A. (2018a). '"Along Kingdom's Highway": The proliferation of Christianity, education, and print amongst the Nagas in Northeast India'. *Contemporary South Asia*: 27(2): 160–178. DOI: 10.1080/09584935.2018.1471041

Longkumer, A. (2018b). 'Bible, guns and land: Sovereignty and nationalism amongst the Nagas of India'. *Nations and Nationalism* 24(4): 1097–1116. DOI: 10.1111/nana.12405.

Longkumer, A. (2018c). '"Nagas can't sit lotus style": Baba Ramdev, Patanjali, and Neo-Hindutva'. *Contemporary South Asia* 26(4): 400–420.

Maaker, E.D., Kikon, D., and Barbora, S. (2016). 'Shifting ground? State and market in the uplands of Northeast India'. *The Newsletter: Encouraging Knowledge and the Study of Asia* 73: 6–7.

Manchanda, R. and Bose, T. (2011). 'Expanding the middle space in the Naga peace process'. *Economic & Political Weekly* 46(53): 51–53.

Manchanda, R. and Kakran, S. (2017). 'Gendered power transformations in India's Northeast: Peace politics in Nagaland'. *Cultural Dynamics* 29(1): 63–82. DOI: 10.1177/0921374017709232.

Mathur, N. (2010). 'Shopping malls, credit cards and global brands: Consumer culture and lifestyle of India's new middle class'. *South Asia Research* 30(3): 211–231. DOI: 10.1177/02627280100300301.

McDuie-Ra, D. (2012a). 'Cosmopolitan tribals: Frontier migrants in Delhi'. *South Asia Research* 32(1): 39–55. DOI: 10.1177/026272801203200103.

McDuie-Ra, D. (2012b). *Northeast migrants in Delhi.* Amsterdam: Amsterdam University Press.

McDuie-Ra, D. (2012c). 'Violence against women in the militarized Indian frontier: Beyond "Indian culture" in the experiences of ethnic minority women'. *Violence Against Women* 18(3): 322–45. DOI: 10.1177/1077801212443114.

McDuie-Ra, D. (2015). '"Is India racist?": Murder, migration and Mary Kom'. *South Asia: Journal of South Asian Studies* 28(2): 304–319. DOI: 10.1080/00856401.2014.992508.

McDuie-Ra, D. (2016a). 'Adjacent identities in Northeast India'. *Asian Ethnicity* 17(3): 400–413. DOI: 10.1080/14631369.2015.1091654

McDuie-Ra, D. (2016b). *Borderland city in New India: Frontier to gateway*. Amsterdam: Amsterdam University Press.

Nielsen, K.B. and Wilhite, H. (2015). 'The rise and fall of the "people's car": Middle-class aspirations, status and mobile symbolism in "New India"'. *Contemporary South Asia* 23(4): 371–387. DOI: 10.1080/09584935.2015.1090951.

Osella, F. and Osella, C. (1999). 'From transience to immanence: Consumption, life-cycle and social mobility in Kerala, South India'. *Modern Asian Studies* 33(4): 989–1020.

Ramakrishnan, K. (2014). 'Cosmopolitan imaginaries on the margins: Negotiating difference and belonging in a Delhi resettlement colony'. *Contemporary South Asia* 22(1): 67–81. DOI: 10.1080/09584935.2013.870976.

Sema, G.P. (2018). 'Political elite and their roles in Nagaland'. *International Journal of Advance Research, Ideas and Innovations in Technology* 4(5): 714–718.

Shankar Das, Y. (2019). 'Why women dominate the entire intellectual spectrum in Nagaland'. Available at: https://timesofindia.indiatimes.com/city/kohima/why-women-dominate-the-entire-intellectual-spectrum-in-nagaland/articleshow/71181512.cms (accessed 19 September 2019).

Shimray, U.A. (2002). 'Equality as tradition: Women's role in Naga society'. *Economic & Political Weekly* 37(5): 375–377. DOI: 10.1245/s10434-015-4688-8.

von Fürer-Haimendorf, C. (1972). 'Recent developments in Nagaland and the northeast frontier agency'. *Asian Affairs* 3(1): 3–13. DOI: 10.1080/03068377208729599.

Walter, N., Bourgois, P., and Loinaz, H.M. (2004). 'Masculinity and undocumented labor migration: Injured Latino day laborers in San Francisco'. *Social Science and Medicine* 59(6): 1159–1168. DOI: 10.1016/j.socscimed.2003.12.013.

Wouters, J.J.P. (2015). 'Polythetic democracy'. *HAU: Journal of Ethnographic Theory* 5(2): 121–151.

Yadav, A. and Shinde, S. (2015). 'Understanding rural to urban migration: Through the case of Nagaland'. In: *National Conference on Urban Issues and Architectural Interventions*, 2015.

Zabiliute, E. (2016). 'Wandering in a mall: Aspirations and family among young urban poor men in Delhi'. *Contemporary South Asia* 24(3): 271–284. DOI: 10.1080/09584935.2016.1208638.

5   'Spinsters and Divorced Women'

'Bad things happened'

Abstract

Chapter 5 discusses the complex gendered contestations occurring within the Naga community as the state opens up to new political ideals, new cultural norms, and new challenges to long-held patriarchal gender norms. The chapter also explores the ways agitations for equal representation contend with a rigidly gendered social order that, as Nagaland's various borders soften and become more porous, is seen by many as a distinct cornerstone of Naga identity.

Keywords: patriarchy, backlash, gender

In April 2016 I travelled with members of a local civil society group from Dimapur to the Nagaland State Vigilance Commissioner's office in Kohima. We were hoping to submit a Right-to-Information request to the Commissioner's office regarding a road being built through a farm near Dimapur. Unrelated to our case, the night before, a violent attack had occurred near the Dimapur train station. A Naga woman was sexually assaulted and subsequently dumped barely clothed on one side of the overpass, about 100 metres east of the station. It was not the first time that a woman had been dumped in that spot in recent history. Halfway through the three-hour drive, we stopped to drink tea and eat at a roadside teashop. We discussed the news, including the assault from the night before.

While our first cups of tea were being poured, we discussed the dangerous nature of the area at night – the poor lighting underneath the overpass, the sparse foot-traffic in many of the surrounding streets after dark, and the high crime rates already reported surrounding the train station. Dimapur train station is notorious as a high-risk area, where bag-snatching is common and where several kidnappings and abductions have occurred in recent history. While there is a police presence in the train station and occasionally in the

Wilkinson, Matthew: *Borderland Anxieties. Shifting Understandings of Gender, Place and Identity at the India-Burma Border.* Amsterdam: Amsterdam University Press, 2023
DOI: 10.5117/9789463729789_CH05

parking lot attached to the train station, the streets surrounding the station are rarely patrolled by police, and the poorly lit areas under the overpass are patrolled even less.

As our second cups of tea arrived, questions about the woman's reasons for being in that area at night were raised, why she was travelling alone, and whether she was knowingly putting herself at risk being near the station after dark. Although the only evidence available was that the woman was left near the overpass, and there was no information in newspapers about where the woman might have been abducted or picked up from, my discussion partners had decided that if the woman was not near the station or overpass originally she must have been in the general area. My partners rhetorically asked each other, 'Why did she go there alone? Everybody knows it's the dangerous part of town' and exclaimed, 'There are taxis and autos [three-wheeler taxis] at the station, if she was going somewhere, she could have taken one'. Whether the woman's attackers were Naga or not Naga was never questioned by my discussion partners. They had decided that she had been attacked by Indian men, who were assumed to be members of the Assam Rifles. This assumption was not baseless. Attacks by Indian paramilitaries on Naga women and women in other 'disturbed areas' of Northeast India are common, and that particular part of Dimapur, near the station, hosts a large army presence.

Our discussion grew heated, and well into our third cups of tea, my partners were becoming animated, slapping their hands on the table and raising their voices. I noticed some of the other people in the teashop turning their heads to see what the fuss was about. The discussion had shifted from initial concerns with the safety of the area at night to assertions that the woman was careless for being in the area alone and speculations that she might have been drinking or had otherwise left herself vulnerable to attack. A section of the overpass near the station is also reputed to be Dimapur's red light district, which added to their speculations and suspicions of the woman's reasons for being near the station alone after dark. One of the discussants exclaimed, 'She left out at night, and then bad things happened, what did she think?' The tone of the conversation was that the woman chose to be in a dangerous place for women at night, with poor lighting and no police. The area has an unsavoury reputation, associated with drugs, alcohol, and prostitution. The responsibility for the attack was laid on her.

In many ways the conversation had similarities with victim-blaming rhetoric that follows violent assaults against women in any city. It is not uncommon for victims of violent attacks, especially sexual attacks, to have the responsibility heaped on themselves, often being accused of carelessness

or even of encouraging their attackers through salacious dress and by giving off 'rape signs' inviting an attack (Kikon, 2015). In light of a string of
highly publicized assaults including the 2012 Delhi rape case, this rhetoric
is particularly common in South Asia, especially in Nagaland and other
'disturbed' areas of India where sexual violence is often associated with
conflict and cultures of impunity (Kikon, 2015, 2016). Although the discussion
was disagreeable and off-putting, there was nothing that was especially
surprising or unusual about its tone or content. However, the discussion
raised themes that also surfaced in other discussions about men, women,
and social order in Nagaland, and these themes were not limited to issues
surrounding sexual violence. Understandings that the public domain is for
Naga men, that Naga women belong in the home and attached to home duties,
and that these rigid gender roles and spaces should not be transgressed
permeated into other aspects of life in Nagaland. For example, in Phek
District several weeks after the discussion described above, I sat in on a
Village Development Board (VDB) meeting. VDBs in Nagaland reserve 25
per cent of seats for women (Government of Nagaland, 1989: 4(b)), yet these
reservations seem to have done little to ameliorate the gendered nature of
decision-making in Naga villages. Men in the meeting discussed budgets
and debated which local roads needed re-laying the most, while the two
women invited to the meeting served food and tea and otherwise sat quietly
throughout. Months after the VDB meeting, James, a politician in Kohima,
mentioned that politics were not a woman's place in Nagaland, and that men
held a 'strength' that was suited for 'doing politics'. In other words, in Naga
society there is a widely accepted understanding of a natural gender order
marked by rigid assertions of men as inhabiting social roles as guardians
and decision-makers in the public sphere, and women as relegated to passive
roles in the private sphere. When women step outside of these roles and
these spaces, vague 'bad things' are thought to be inevitable consequences.
These 'bad things' may range from being abducted and attacked when in
areas that women are not supposed to be in or at times women should not
be out, according to their self-selected male watchers, to larger disruptions
of tradition to and the destabilization of Naga society.

In this chapter, I engage with emerging challenges to these rigidly
gendered understandings of politics and life in Nagaland and, in doing
so, I build on my argument that post-conflict changes in Nagaland have
encouraged new contestations and assertions of gender and identity at the
border. In the wake of ceasefire, women in Nagaland are becoming more
economically empowered and more independent. In many households in
Nagaland the woman may be the sole breadwinner. Men in Nagaland do

continue to be the centre of political life, but this once established norm and the idea of 'equality as tradition' is challenged now more than it ever was. Naga women are making calls for rights to take part in politics and to own ancestral land, and a patriarchal backlash is taking place in Nagaland in response to these changes. The patriarchal backlash takes the form of amplified support for highly patriarchal customary institutions and for men's continued dominance of politics in Nagaland. These issues are linked to customary traditions and cultural and indigenous rights and involve resistance to women's efforts for political and land-ownership rights, vehement defence of patriarchal customary traditions and institutions, and increased surveillance and management of the movements and relationships of Naga women. This is significant, because looking at the ways post-conflict changes in Nagaland have encouraged a patriarchal backlash offers an insight into the ways that the liberalization of the borderland encourages new forms of contestation and conflict along gendered lines. This chapter is divided into three sections. In the first section, I discuss the ways land, patrilineal traditions, and customary institutions are embodied in a widely understood sense of 'equality as tradition'. Following this, I discuss women's pushes for political involvement in the state since ceasefire, and the backlash to women's increased participation in politics and the labour force. Finally, I discuss the ways Nagaland's patriarchal backlash can be understood as a wider effort to protect indigenous traditions in a post-conflict borderland that is facing immense economic, social, and political changes, where rigidly gendered traditions are seen by many as a fragile and essential piece of ethnic identity.

(In)equality as Tradition

The younger people, they are educated now ... they want this development. They go outside, to Bangalore, to Delhi, to Dubai, to Europe, Australia, and they see how it is there. They hear all these things, different to the village and different from customs, and they want that development. They don't want old men telling them what to do ... But, also, this is tradition. This is who we are, as Nagas. They need to respect that, their elders. It's what we've had to fight for, for our rights ... This is my house. My property. Yes, my ama[1] lives here, but my father left this to me. I have to keep this, for the future. The man and the woman have roles to play,

1   Mother.

and the man here, is to guard this for the future [pointing at the linoleum floor]. That's what the younger people won't understand. They want it all now. It's about future this thing.[2]

While interviewing men in several smaller 'Roxy'[3] dens in Dimapur between 2016 and 2020, discussions often turned to a generational gap in Nagaland, a gap marked by differing values, differing aspirations, and a cautious balance between conservative tribal and Christian values marked by respect for elders, the maintenance of traditions, and rigidly drawn lines between acceptable and unacceptable behaviours and lifestyles. Isaac, mentioned above, exemplifies the wider attitude that many Naga men hold towards the emerging questions and challenges towards Nagaland's rigidly gendered social models. As Isaac alludes to, the maintenance of these highly patriarchal traditions is attached to the defence and maintenance of indigenous rights, which since the loss of popular support for Naga independence has become much more contested within the Naga community. Isaac, aged in his mid-forties, regularly came to the Roxy dens to buy cheap scotch and local rice wine, which he preferred to drink at home. He described himself as 'educated unemployed' when I inquired about what he does for a living, which was a common scenario for many of the men drinking in Roxy dens. While making small talk about my reasons for being in Nagaland, Isaac invited me to visit him at his house in the north of the city. Isaac and I discussed changes in the city since the 1990s, and Isaac's perspective of the future of Nagaland amid some of the changes that have taken place since the 1990s. Isaac's answers betrayed a common sentiment among men in similar positions surrounding legacies, respect, and rigid gender roles. The discussion with Isaac, although brief, reflected similar discussions I have had in Nagaland since 2012. Isaac held firmly to a model of respect that is rooted in gendered roles of protection and guarding land for the future. Nagaland is undergoing significant change in the wake of ceasefire. Some of these changes, as discussed in Chapter 4, involve the state 'opening up', and new opportunities presented to an emerging post-conflict middle class. Many of these opportunities offer Naga women in particular new freedoms, mobilities, and forms of empowerment. The 'issue' of youth, as Isaac and many of the other men I held discussions with in the state, is that a population of Nagas, often being but not necessarily young, seek forms of empowerment and

2   Interview, December 2019.
3   Local rice wine.

representation that defy this rigidly gendered model of a 'traditional' Naga society, one where men have representative and decision-making authority and where women, although independent in many senses, do not have an equal stake in land ownership, in family and tribe legacies, and in the future of Naga society.

Naga customary institutions, patrilineal traditions, and land are inextricably linked. Naga men are held in high-regard as leaders, guardians, and custodians of Naga territory, culture, and society, and are seen as naturally adept to carry the legacies of their respective tribes and clans. Land is an integral part of these legacies and to the survival of tribe and clan groups. Land is the anchor of identity, it is an integral part of one's clan, family, and village (Jamir, 2014). Even for Nagas who may have been born outside of or live far away from their ancestral lands, identity is closely tied to one's home village and any plots of land that family in the village owns. Owning land, especially in one's home village, is an integral aspect of of identity and is central to a rigidly gendered understanding of Naga society. Naga men own land on behalf of their families and ancestors, and keeping this land is a crucial part of maintaining links to tribe, clan, and family identity (Karlsson and Kikon, 2017). Naga women are attached to their respective tribes, clans, and villages through the dominant men in their lives, typically fathers or husbands. The prevailing ideology is that through women's changing attachments to tribes, clans and villages, land can be lost to other tribes and clans. Essentially men are the embodiments of tribe and clan identities, and women are liabilities through which ancestral property can be lost to other tribes and clans following marriage. The rigid compartmentalization of gender roles and responsibilities, where men act as heads of their clans, villages, and households, and where women are tethered to the identities of their fathers and later to their husbands is commonly referred to as 'equality as tradition'. Equality as tradition reflects perceptions that men have a natural propensity towards leadership and 'serious issues' such as managing land and resources and conducting warfare, and that women are naturally destined for roles associated with maintaining the household, raising children, and supporting and obeying the men in their lives. This is sometimes also referred to as men being 'heads of the household' and women as being 'heads of the kitchen'. References to equality as tradition are typically followed by a list of positive indicators of women's empowerment and independence in the state relative to Indian indicators. These include substantiated and unsubstantiated claims that Naga women have higher rates of literacy than women in other parts of India, that Naga women are more likely to be gainfully employed, that female foeticide and gender-based abortions do not occur in Nagaland, that Naga society does not having a dowry system, and that eve teasing[4] does not happen in Nagaland and that Naga men do not eve tease. Some of these claims, such as Naga women having higher rates of literacy than women in other parts of India may be based in fact, while other claims are difficult to prove, obviously exaggerated, or simply incorrect. For example, one discussant, 'Esther' offered an illustration of Naga customary institutions taking action on gendered violence, stating that 'if a husband is beating his wife, fighting, hitting, hitting, then the village council will come and tell him not to do it again, make sure he doesn't do it again ... She will be protected'. Despite widely known violence against women in Nagaland, committed from outside and inside the Naga community, discussions of equality as tradition are rife with clarifications that Naga women are more empowered than in other parts of India and are given protection under Naga customary law. This arrangement is seen as a reflection of innate strengths and weaknesses attached to gender. In other words, equality as tradition is rooted in ideas that men and women in Nagaland are considered equal, that Naga women are treated better than women are in other parts of India, and women have consideration, but not representation, in issues of governance and community decision-making. One discussant, Francis, described this ethic with reference to village labour and an idea of married men and women forming a 'whole':

> You have to see, women and men, we're different people. Men can do the harder tasks, really harder, chopping, building, making. We used to be head-hunters, warring always. Women don't have that strength. They are for other things. In Naga traditions, women have rights, much more than in other places, but it has to be a balance. The man can't go out to work, all day, hard work, like in village, and then cooking, cleaning, while the wife does nothing. Not working. They have respect, they have their rights, but a husband and wife make a whole. Each has a strength.

In the two decades since ceasefire, as Nagaland's economy undergoes a post-conflict boom, as the state opens up to new forms of engagement with India and surrounding countries, and as new opportunities are presented to a younger generation of Naga women, new questions have been raised

---

4   'Eve teasing' is a euphemism used throughout South Asia to refer to common acts of public sexual harassment, most often committed by men towards women, that include leering, making sexually suggestive gestures and remarks, and unwanted physical contact. Misri (2011) offers a discussion of the term 'Eve Teasing' and its roots.

about women's place in Naga society. Women in Nagaland are becoming more independent and are playing a greater role in Nagaland's economic and political landscape. Naga women are more able to earn their own incomes, often taking on entrepreneurial pursuits at home in the borderland or thriving in larger Indian cities where Naga men face more difficulties (see McDuie-Ra, 2012b). In many households the woman has become the primary breadwinner, while husbands, brothers, or uncles struggle to find work or have given up the prospects of getting work altogether. Despite these new opportunities, rigid social norms continue to apply inside and outside the household. As Manchanda and Kakran (2017: 74) argue, 'this generation of professional women create wealth and are blocked by the men of the clan from disposing of it'. One discussant, Tabitha, is illustrative of this situation. Tabitha lives with her younger brothers in her family home. Her parents have both died, leaving the house to the eldest brother according to custom. As both brothers have not found work, Tabitha has had to take on work in a local shop. Besides her shop work, she occasionally takes on catering jobs for friends and family for a small fee. In Tabitha's words:

> I have to do it all … I get up at 4, I have to do the cooking, keep the house together, I do the cleaning. Then, I'm the one that works. I come home, I make the lunch, then more housework. If it's people coming, who prepares? I do it. It's just exhausting.

Tabitha's case is not exceptional or unusual. While the state's opening up has brought new opportunities for work to the borderland, as discussed in the previous chapter, there continues to be a pervasive sense that 'real' work is done by Naga men. 'Real work' often means government work, which has traditionally been much more secure in a state with a small economy and few secure livelihood options. Government work is highly competitive, but when found brings status and security. Hence, men will often wait for opportunities to be presented for government work, whether that is waiting to take the Civil Service Exam in the state or seeking alternative ways to enter into the government workforce. Alternative pathways may include seeking out or waiting for influential friends and family to help gain-entry into a government office. Women also work for Nagaland state government, and it needs to be made clear that taking some form of government-entry exam is common practice for high school graduates throughout the state. However, with less pressure to find a government job than men traditionally have faced, women in Nagaland are more likely to take on work that is available. Not having the security of political representation, or of owning ancestral lands, has meant many Naga women have had to find their own forms of empowerment in the emerging post-conflict economy, in higher education, or have left Nagaland to seek better alternatives elsewhere (Shankar Das, 2019). In some cases, mostly limited to Nagaland's larger urban hubs, women have inherited property from parents and elder relatives, although this is limited to newly acquired property and not ancestral land (Shankar Das, 2018). Essentially, as women in Nagaland do find employment either in the borderland, or outside in larger Indian cities, rigidly gendered social and political traditions face new challenges. As these women take on a greater role in a market economy that is increasingly important in Naga society and as they engage with ideas of democracy and citizenship outside of the state, demands for equal rights and political representation have grown.

Private land in Nagaland is managed under Article 371A of India's Constitution and the Nagaland Government Land and Revenue Regulation (Amendment) Act 1978. Article 371(A) of the Constitution of India grants special powers to Naga customary institutions, stating that no Act of Parliament 'in respect of the ownership and transfer of land and its resources, shall apply to the State of Nagaland unless the Legislative Assembly of Nagaland by a resolution so decides'. Communal land, including common village land comprising graveyards, community platforms, churches, monuments, and reserved forests; clan land comprising specific plots of land allotted to clan groups; and lineage land, a sub-division of clan land allotted to families. Communal land is managed at the village level by Naga customary institutions, including village councils and chieftainships. While these policies aim to prevent land being sold or leased to non-Nagas, the mechanisms are contested and everyday exchanges of land are managed through village-based decision-making bodies. While these customary institutions differ between tribes, clans, and villages, they do share some common characteristics. Primarily, with few exceptions these institutions are either restricted to men or are overwhelmingly dominated by men (Khutso, 2018: 146–147). In many villages women are forbidden to enter the Morung where men discuss politics and make decisions on behalf of clans and villages. In some villages women are not allowed within a particular distance of the Morung (Manchanda and Kakran, 2017). In some villages women do have access to decision-making institutions however that access is often limited to watching and listening in on discussions while being discouraged from speaking or taking part, and often also involves providing food and tea to male decision-makers. Other land takes the form of individual landholdings held by individuals and families but is also subject to the laws of village councils and customary institutions, especially regarding rules of exchange and inheritance. Long established patrilineal traditions determine that men can inherit individual ancestral lands but women cannot (Hutton, 1921: 137). A Naga woman may construct a house, and may buy land, however upon marriage those become the property of her husband (Niumai, 2015: 357). If a husband and wife divorce, according to customary traditions, the children and property belong to the husband. When the father dies, land is divided between sons, or if the father has daughters, between the next male heirs in his lineage – brothers, cousins, or other male relatives. These patrilineal traditions emerge from a rigidly gendered social order where men carry the legacies of tribes, clans, and families, while women's identities and legacies are tethered to those of their fathers or husbands.

Patriarchal Backlash

> It's controversial to say it, but this feminism, everywhere, all over the world, it's not good. All these riots, problems, pushing for change, it's all because of this feminism. In Nagaland we can't have it, can't allow it. Of course, to you, you're a Westerner, it sounds so primitive, but you can see it too. But with all this feminism, all this political [sic] correct, it can't fit here. Naga women have the rights, and they are respected here. But it's a tribal system, we're an indigenous people, this isn't like Delhi, or in the West, not like in that way.[5]

Challenges to Nagaland's customary institutions and norms have met with vehement and violent resistance. Resistance to change to Nagaland's customary institutions came to a head in 2017 over women's reservations for Urban Local Bodies (ULBs). Starting in 2011, the Gauhati (Guwahati) High Court made efforts to pressure Nagaland State Government to hold ULB polls within the requirements of Article 234(T) of India's Constitution, that is, reserving 33 per cent of ULB seats for women. While this require-ment had been postponed on request of the Government of Nagaland, in April 2016 the court admitted a petition, filed by members of the Naga Mothers Association contending that Article234(T) did extend to Nagaland. In November 2016, following pressure from the Gauhati High Court, the Nagaland State Assembly revoked its earlier opposition to Article 243(T) of India's Constitution, requiring municipal bodies reserve 33 per cent of seats

5   Interview, November 2019.

for women. This was widely read as Article 234(T) superseding Nagaland's constitutionally protected autonomy enshrined in Article 371(A) of India's constitution. Throughout the High Court deliberations tensions flared in Nagaland. Any rules reserving seats for women, in any political body, were viewed as contravening Article 371(A) and upsetting Nagaland's long held patriarchal customary traditions. On 31 January 2017, two youths in Dimapur were killed by police firing while protesting the enforced reservations, and twelve others were injured. On 2 February, violence erupted throughout Nagaland in response to the High Court's decision and motivated by the two deaths. Naga civil society groups opposing the High Court's decision blockaded streets and rampaged through Kohima, Dimapur, and several other urban centres throughout the state. In the ensuing violence twenty-one government buildings were burned down and eleven vehicles were set alight. Nagaland's Chief Minister, T.R. Zeliang, was forced to resign as a result of the protests. The Civic Body Elections were postponed indefinitely.

The protests were a response to a perceived overstep of Indian law into Nagaland. There were and continue to be widespread fears that the protections granted to Nagaland's customary politics under Article 371(A) are tenuous and under attack. However, the extreme violence associated with resisting women's pushes for political inclusion in Nagaland was also a response to a perceived challenge to traditional notions of a rigidly gendered Naga social order. Dhillon's (2017) interviews with Naga men and women in Kohima in the week following the February riot brought to surface a consensus among several Naga conservatives that the pushes for Article 243(T) were led by 'trouble-making' women, 'spinsters' and 'divorced women' who have been influenced by outside actors. Furthermore, protests and riots took place in rural areas of the state that were not subject to the ULB elections, and in parts of Nagaland that were not having elections. Several tribal bodies held the Naga Mothers Association responsible for the deaths and the protests, arguing that women's agitations for political change had triggered the initial violence (Parashar, 2017). The protests were a reflection of a wider patriarchal backlash that has been taking place in Nagaland since women's pushes for greater political have accelerated in the late 1990s and early 2000s and are seen as threatening to a number of institutions.

This patriarchal backlash is not limited to spectacular outbursts of organized violence. It occurs in a number of spaces, from state-level policy making to household and kitchen politics. It varies in form but is often performed through chastising women who speak out against patriarchal traditions or who speak in favour of inclusive change. The patriarchal backlash involves, among other practices, ex-communicating women who overstep their traditional roles as non-speaking and non-political subjects. This is especially visible in Nagaland's eastern towns and villages. For example, in 2017, eight women in Phek District were excommunicated and banished from their villages for defying the community's January ULB resolution and attempting to contest seats in Urban Local Bodies. As well as ex-communicating women who overstep traditional gender roles and chastising outspoken women, the patriarchal backlash involves intensive efforts to monitor, police, and control the movements and relationships of Naga women. In doing so, the nexus between outsiders, identity, Naga women, and land is made clear. Discussed in the following chapter, women who defy traditions of having relationships and marrying within the Naga community, and instead form relationships with and/or marry outsiders, especially those of Bengali or Bangladeshi heritage, are subject to intense social rapprochement and ostracism. In other words, by exercising greater forms of independence and overstepping rigidly cast roles as docile, obedient, and non-speaking subjects, by leaving the kitchen, Naga women face a patriarchal backlash that threatens their security and, ultimately, their identity as Naga.

There are other contributing factors to the patriarchal backlash in Nagaland. There are men and women in Nagaland who defend patriarchal politics and rigid gender norms and recognize these forms as a reflection of an ideal Naga society and as key components of Naga identity. There are also elites and conservatives who benefit from Nagaland's customary arrangements, and for whom changes to these arrangements may threaten their political empowerment, may reduce or dissolve opportunities to personally benefit from licit and illicit economies, and may threaten their social status. Conservatives and elites, however, are often already in empowered positions, and liberalization offers opportunities to many of these actors to further exploit opportunities associated with new markets for land and resources. Wouters (2018) has discussed in-depth the economics of Nagaland's ceasefire politics, where elites profiteer enormously as gatekeepers to the state for local communities. Likewise, Karlsson (2011) discussed the ways elites in neighbouring Meghalaya profiteer as gatekeepers to the state's resources for outsiders. Alongside changes in the state that are perceived to threaten fundamental institutions, and ultimately, are perceived to be threats to the survival of Naga society, the idea of equality as tradition perpetuates a popular idea of a natural and ideal gendered order in Nagaland. Those who challenge this order are often assumed to misunderstand their own histories and to have been corrupted by outside ideas of Western feminism that are at odds with traditional understandings of Naga society.

These issues have gained prominence at a time of great change in Naga-land. In the wake of ceasefire, as the state opens up, as markets expand, and as new possibilities are presented to a generation of younger Nagas, Nagas and especially Naga women are transgressing their traditionally gendered roles and spaces. Women in Nagaland are increasingly economically empowered, are exercising greater agency over their lives, and are agitating for political access and property rights. Anxieties among Naga conservatives that these changes spell 'bad things' in the future abound. These bad things include the destruction of Naga cultural traditions, the loss of land and by extension the loss of identity, and ultimately to the state of Nagaland being overwhelmed by non-Nagas and Nagas becoming a minority in their own state. Overall, Nagaland's patriarchal backlash is a response to a number of anxieties surrounding the future of the state, as long held patterns of land use are disrupted by expanding markets, as traditional gender constructions are challenged by new opportunities presented to women in Nagaland, and as an influx of outsiders coming into the state are perceived to threaten Naga hegemony in the state. This occurs in the midst of a growing crisis of masculinity, where many Naga men feel emasculated under a disempowering military occupation and Naga women are exercising greater degrees of economic empowerment, independence, and have more agency in their life decisions. Furthermore, ideas that agitators for inclusive change are corrupted or are otherwise influenced from the outside are a popular refrain to calls for change. Because of this, a new and mutually exclusive binary has emerged in Nagaland, between inclusive feminist models of citizenship, and the essence of what it means to be Naga.

Various iterations of patriarchal backlash have been discussed in gender and masculinity literature. Faludi (1991) coined the term when describing a counterassault in popular media, as well as in political administrations, against women's rights movements in the United States in the 1970s and 1980s. According to Faludi (1991) a patriarchal backlash was motivated by a women's liberation movement that successfully breached traditional 'women's spaces' and encouraged women to transgress home-based roles. Faludi's (1991) 'backlash' hypothesis postulates that when women take non-traditional roles, there is a trend of resistance through media, in politics, and at the household level in an attempt to 'resubjugate' women. Other studies have provided some support for this hypothesis. Avakame (1999) found that the backlash hypothesis offers a compelling explanation for increased rates of violence against women as women's participation in the workforce increases. Ethnographic studies have provided further insight into this backlash violence. One of the most widely cited examples is Guttman's (1996) ethnography of Mexican *Machismo* cultures, lending in-depth insight into the ways men in Mexico City use violence against other men and against women to retain and regain control in a context where men are less secure in terms of employment and fulfilling social masculine ideals, and where women are exercising greater agency and independence. Likewise, Carrington and Scott (2008) found that amid 'sweeping social changes to rural life', men in rural Australia, an interior borderland in many senses, 'resort to violence as a largely strategic practice deployed to recreate an imagined rural gender order' (Carrington and Scott, 2008: 641). While, on the whole, violence against women is negatively correlated with rising women's wages and economic activity (Christy-McMullin, 2006; Vieraitis et al., 2015), in cases where women transcend established gender norms and become more independent and more empowered than the men in their lives, especially husbands, de-facto partners, and siblings, that a backlash takes place in the form of domestic violence, stringent checks and controls over movements, and increased surveillance of women has wide consensus (Carrington and Scott, 2008; Hunnicutt, 2009; Morrell et al., 2012).

Despite the insights offered by the literature above, literature discussing patriarchal backlash is narrow in its understanding of violence and the agents of violence. Literature typically focuses on men's individual acts of violence at the household level. Intimate partner violence, especially as women in households find work, enjoy increased incomes and to some degree become more independent, has dominated discussions of patriarchal backlash (Hautzinger, 2003). These discussions reflect the tenets of Messerschmidt's (2005) hypothesis that violence may be employed as a means of reversing subordinations of masculinity. Overall, the argument is that the patriarchal backlash is a masculine response to challenges by women against established gender norms within the household itself. Less is known, however, about the ways men respond to wider institutional shifts in political and gendered orders on a greater societal scale. In other words, the ways men and women collectively respond to transgressions of gender norms that displace local patriarchal structures. While Connell (1995: 82) argues that 'a gender order where men dominate women cannot avoid constituting men as an interest group concerned with defence, and women as an interest group concerned with change', this change is much more complex than men feeling threatened by women staking a greater control over household resources and exercising some forms of employment-linked independence. Hautzinger (2003: 93) recognizes this complexity, stating that 'insecurities linked to masculinities are not just about the erosion of male status, power, or identity, but the way in which gendered aspects of social organization are structurally threatened by much larger historical destabilizations, and the complex psycho-social reactions of men to these events'. In other words, the patriarchal backlash not only stems from women's empowerment relative to men at the household level, but encompasses wider disruptions to established gender norms, concerns about identity and ethnicity, and attachments to gendered systems which, while being oppressive, provide a clear sense of purpose and place. Melo Lopes (2018) refers to this as a post-feminist backlash, marked by enforcement of patriarchal gender norms by men and women onto any person breaching these well-established norms.

Backlash is especially relevant to borderlands and post-conflict sites. Borderlands and conflict/post-conflict sites are highly gendered spaces, where the presence of conflict often serves to further embed patriarchies, discourage the movement and public involvement of women, and inform hyper-masculine constructions that normalize men's violence in a number of domains. As borderlands and conflict/post-conflict sites change, especially through the expansion of markets and liberalization in the borderland, patriarchal structures and systems are increasingly being questioned and challenged. As such, responses to changing gender norms, the transgression of pre-existing norms, and challenges to rigidly gendered resource control regimes are magnified at these sites. The ways patriarchal backlash takes place in the borderland suggest that backlash is closely tied to wider social changes, anxieties, and insecurities. Some research indicates that this may be the case, that patriarchal backlash may be closely linked to wider insecurities and anxieties surrounding masculinity, control, and disempowerment. Nagaland's patriarchal backlash offers new insights into these understandings of backlash. In the wake of ceasefire many patriarchal norms and customs are being questioned and challenged by groups within the state, such as Naga women, and groups outside of the state, namely, the Government of India. This takes place in a context where decades of militarization and economic stagnation, although changing, leaves limited avenues for Naga men to satisfy masculine norms involving finding and keeping work and acting as guardians of Naga territory, culture, and society from outside incursions. Aptly stated by Manchanda (2004: n.p):

> In a society that traditionally was locked in endemic war cycles (involving headhunting) male value was marked by the physical prowess to fight. The protracted experience of living under the virtual rule of the Indian security, has emasculated Naga men's self-perception of their role as protectors. There is a crisis of 'masculinity' that is reinforced by the opening up of new roles of agency for women. It also predicates a backlash.

Understanding the deeper roots of Nagaland's patriarchal backlash, the ways that defence of patriarchal institutions is attached to changing land use patterns, women's agitations for land rights, and the perceived influx of outsiders in the state, offers insights into the ways change at the post-conflict borderland encourages new forms and new justifications for patriarchy and subjugation, and ultimately, forms of violence that emerge from change. Nagaland's patriarchal backlash is closely tied to efforts to preserve indigenous rights, embodied in patriarchal customary institutions and a rigidly gendered understanding of Naga society. A change to one is seen as a threat to the other. The legacies of conflict in the state, involving the state's ongoing militarization are reminders of the tentative position of Naga society. Changes in the state in the wake of ceasefire, as discussed in Chapters 5 and 6, have in many ways further upset Naga cultural norms and a narrowly drawn understanding of what Naga society is. In light of these changes, patriarchal norms in Nagaland are considered by many as a stable bedrock of Naga society that cannot be compromised, and hence, when challenged, attracts a widespread and violent backlash.

Conclusion

This chapter began with a conversation about an assault that occurred in Dimapur in 2016. A Naga woman had been sexually attacked in the night and dumped unconscious near the town's train station at an overpass, a site where other women were said to have been dumped before. The discussion began with concerns about Dimapur's poor security situation and the problematic infrastructure that leaves parts of the town dark and poorly patrolled by police at night. Within minutes, however, the discussion had swayed to concerns of why the woman was alone in that part of town after dark. By the end of the discussion, the focus had shifted again, to the woman's carelessness and suspicions that she may have been drunk, may have been a prostitute, or may have otherwise been putting herself at risk. The general theme that the discussion ended on was that the woman had been in a dangerous place at a dangerous time, and if she had stayed in her home or had travelled with a male guardian, harm would not have come to her. By stepping outside of her home she had taken a risk and had been assaulted and dumped near the overpass as a result. My discussants alluded that the sexual assault was a punishment for the woman's transgression, for being somewhere that she should not have been. The overarching ethic of the discussion was that when Naga women step outside of their pre-ordained spaces and roles, as one discussant pointed out, 'bad things happen'. This ethic was not limited to the case of the sexual assault, however. The themes that surfaced in this discussion, of rigid gendered roles and spaces, of risks associated with women's exercises of independence and agency, and of a perverse justice for transgressions of these roles resurfaced in numerous conversations and interactions in Nagaland. Rigidly gendered understandings of Naga society have become new focal points in what many Nagas see as a fight for Naga autonomy and cultural survival in light of these changes. There are a multitude of reasons for this, including fears that extending political rights and property rights to Naga women will eventually place land in the hands of non-Nagas, fears that outsiders are coming into the state and may overwhelm the state, anxieties surrounding the Indian state's attempts to extend its laws into Nagaland, and concerns that Naga women may form relationships with outsiders and 'dilute' Naga bloodlines. The preservation of 'equality as tradition', or as I have named it in this chapter '(In)equality as tradition', is seen as commensurate to the survival of Naga society in general. The prominence and greater emphasis on Naga patriarchal customs and the rigidly gendered cultures that customary institutions espouse is an outcome of anxieties associated with change in the state, and this has led to new assertions and contestations over men's roles in Naga society. The patriarchal backlash emerges from a sense that the rigidly gendered order of Naga society is both fundamental and tenuous. For conservative groups in Nagaland, patriarchy is Naga society, and for men experiencing the state's opening up and the liberalization of the post-conflict borderland, at the edge of India, challenges to patriarchy are commensurate to challenges to the essence of Naga society.

References

Avakame, EF. (1999). 'Females' labor force participation and intimate femicide: An empirical assessment of the backlash hypothesis'. *Violence Against Women* 5(8): 926–949. DOI: 10.1177/10778019922181554.

Carrington, K. and Scott, J. (2008). 'Masculinity, rurality and violence'. *British Journal of Criminology* 48(5): 641–666. DOI: 10.1093/bjc/azn031.

Christy-McMullin, K. (2006). 'An evidence-based approach to a theoretical understanding of the relationship between economic resources, race/ethnicity, and woman abuse'. *Journal of Evidence-Based Social Work* 3(2): 1–30. DOI: 10.1300/J394v03n02.

Connell, R. (1995). *Masculinities*. New York: SAGE Publications.

Dhillon, A. (2017). 'Nagaland, where men are on strike until women go back to the kitchen'. *The Sydney Morning Herald*, 16 February. Sydney.

Faludi, S. (1991). *Backlash: The undeclared war against American women*. New York: Three Rivers Press. DOI: 10.1177/036168439201600304.

Government of Nagaland (1989). Village development boards model rules (Revised). India.

Guttman, M.C. (1996). *The meanings of macho: Being a man in Mexico City*. Berkeley: University of California Press.

Hautzinger, S. (2003). 'Researching men's violence: Personal reflections on ethnographic data'. *Men and Masculinities* 6(1): 93–106. DOI: 10.1177/1097184X03253139.

Hunnicutt, G. (2009). 'Varieties of patriarchy and violence against women: Resurrecting "patriarchy" as a theoretical tool'. *Violence Against Women* 15(5): 553–573.

Hutton, J.H. (1921). *The Angami Nagas: With some notes on neighbouring tribes*. London: Macmillan and Co Ltd.

Jamir, T. (2014). 'Gender land relations in Nagaland: Dilemma of balancing tradition and Modernity'. *International Journal of Gender and Women's Studies* 2(1): 121–133.

Karlsson, B.G. (2011). *Unruly hills: A political ecology of India's Northeast*. Berghahn Books.

Karlsson, B.G. and Kikon, D. (2017). 'Wayfinding: Indigenous migrants in the service sector of metropolitan India'. *South Asia: Journal of South Asia Studies* 40(3). Routledge: 447–462. DOI: 10.1080/00856401.2017.1319145.

Kikon, D. (2015). *Life and dignity: Women's testimonies of sexual violence in Dimapur (Nagaland)*. Guwahati: North Eastern Social Research Centre.

Kikon, D. (2016). 'Memories of rape: The banality of violence and impunity in Naga society'. In: Chakravarti, U. (ed.) *Fault lines of history: The India papers II*. Zubaan. New Delhi.

Manchanda, R. (2004). 'We do more because we can: Naga women in the peace process'. In: *South Asian Forum for Human Rights*, Kathmandu, 2004.

Manchanda, R. and Kakran, S. (2017). 'Gendered power transformations in India's Northeast: Peace politics in Nagaland'. *Cultural Dynamics* 29(1): 63–82. DOI: 10.1177/0921374017709232.

McDuie-Ra, D. (2012b). *Northeast migrants in Delhi*. Amsterdam: Amsterdam University Press.

Melo Lopes, F. (2018). 'Perpetuating the patriarchy: Misogyny and (post-)feminist backlash'. *Philosophical Studies* 176(9): 1–22. DOI: 10.1007/s11098-018-1138-z.

Messerschmidt, J.W. (2005). 'Men, masculinities and crime'. In: Kimmel, M.S., Hearn, J., and Connell, R.W. (eds) *Handbook of studies on men and masculinities*. London: SAGE Publications Inc.

Misri, D. (2011). '"Are you a man?": Performing naked protest in India'. *Signs* 36(3): 603–625. DOI: 10.1163/_afco_asc_2291.

Morrell, R., Jewkes, R., and Lindegger, G. (2012). 'Hegemonic masculinity/masculinities in South Africa: Culture, power, and gender politics'. *Men and Masculinities* 15(1): 11–30. DOI: 10.1177/1097184X12438001.

Niumai, A. (2015). 'Gender among the Nagas of North East India'. In: Pande R (ed.) *Gender lens: Women's issues and perspectives*. New Delhi: Rawat Publisher. DOI: 10.13140/RG.2.1.3743.4402.

Parashar, U. (2017). 'In Nagaland, it's a long march for women's quota in local governments'. *Hindustan Times*, 15 February. New Delhi.

Shankar Das, Y. (2018). 'Denied for centuries, Naga women get right to own land now'. *The Times of India*, 16 August. New Delhi.

Shankar Das, Y. (2019). 'Why women dominate the entire intellectual spectrum in Nagaland'. Available at: https://timesofindia.indiatimes.com/city/kohima/why-women-dominate-the-entire-intellectual-spectrum-in-nagaland/articleshow/71181512.cms (accessed 19 September 2019).

Vieraitis, L.M., Britto, S., and Morris, R.G. (2015). 'Assessing the impact of changes in gender equality on female homicide victimization: 1980–2000'. *Crime & Delinquency* 61(3): 428–453. DOI: 10.1177/0011128711420100.

Wouters, J.J.P. (2018). *In the shadows of Naga insurgency: Tribes, state, and violence in Northeast India*. New Delhi: Oxford University Press.

6   New Politics of Gender at the Border

Abstract
Chapter 6 discusses the ways migration into Nagaland from other parts
of India and from Bangladesh have created an explosive political narrative of 'outsiders' and threats to Nagaland's demographic balance. This
narrative is led by highly gendered notions of Naga men as protectors of
Naga territory, culture, and society from outside intruders.

Keywords: migration, xenophobia, outsiders

'Stop Harbouring IBIs. They are Not Your Family Members'

Between November 2017 and January 2018, a series of five posters were
plastered at intersections, markets, transport hubs and along walls and
buildings in the busier streets of Dimapur and the neighbouring town of
Chümoukedima. The posters, printed in plain white and pastel yellow, blue,
pink and orange, carried various slogans agitating for more stringent checks
on migration into Nagaland, the introduction and enforcement of policies to
restrict migration into Nagaland, and the expulsion of illegal Bangladeshi
migrants in particular. The five variations of the posters were: 'Our fight is
against IBIs [illegal Bangladeshi immigrants] and not against religion'; 'Wake
up Naga's [sic], no time to pretend we have our fundamental rights in our
land'; 'Restore back Inner Line Permit at Dimapur district'; 'State government
you have slept too long, deport illegal Bangladeshi migrants'; and 'It is our
rights to protect our land: [1.] Stop renting out to IBIs. [2.] Stop employing
IBIs. [3.] Stop harbouring IBIs. They are not your family members'. Similar
references to the problem of 'outsiders', and specifically to IBIs, appeared
regularly in local newspapers, in public forums and events, in discussions on
streets, in eateries, and in tea shops. IBIs, often referred to collectively as the
'IBI menace' seemed to be attached to almost all political issues in Nagaland
in some way and were co-opted into various other political problems and
projects. Public forums discussing unemployment and self-employment

Wilkinson, Matthew: *Borderland Anxieties. Shifting Understandings of Gender, Place and Identity
at the India-Burma Border.* Amsterdam: Amsterdam University Press, 2023
DOI: 10.5117/9789463729789_CH06

often segued into discussions of IBIs living in Nagaland and speculations that IBIs were the source of Nagaland's high unemployment rate by offering cheaper labour than locals were willing to work for (Nagaland Post, 2019). Conversations in underground bars and taverns often touched on a popular conspiracy theory that IBIs were trying to take over the state by starting businesses that only hired Bangladeshis, using various forms of trickery to marry Naga women, and ultimately 'breeding out' Nagas in their own state. Violent crimes, especially sexual attacks and rapes, were often initially at least suspected to have been committed by IBIs. Whenever a Naga woman was attacked by a non-Naga who is not an Indian paramilitary, the IBI menace was brought up almost immediately in newspaper opinion pages and in conversations on the street. While these theories were specious, and often were the loud opinions of a few influential and inflammatory community members who had a devoted local following, the rhetoric against IBIs was commonplace and seldom challenged. The IBI, and by extension any outsider who may have looked Bangladeshi, was Muslim, or spoke Bengali was under suspicion. The implications of this environment of suspicion were also very serious. People who are thought to be IBIs have been harassed, and attacked on many occasions by angry crowds of locals, often for suspected sexual attacks or sexual involvement with Naga women (Laskar, 2015; Thyrniang, 2015).

In one particularly dark episode in 2015, Syed Sarifuddin Khan was accused of raping a Naga girl on 23 February. Khan was arrested the following day and held in Dimapur Central Jail. Within a week of the arrest, rumours were quickly spread that Syed Khan was a Bangladeshi immigrant, with one local newspaper, the *Nagaland Post*, running a headline about the alleged rape that read 'IBI rapes woman in DMU [Dimapur]'. The Naga Council Dimapur and the Naga Women's Hoho Dimapur issued a joint statement in several local newspapers, stating that they were 'once again compelled to condemn the rape of a Sumi Naga girl by a suspected IBI. Not only was the girl raped multiple times, she was beaten up and threatened ... Unless all Nagas take responsibility to tackle the menace of an unabated IBI influx ... crimes against our women and daughters by these people will only increase'. On 3 March 2015, the Naga Students' Federation issued a similar statement, condemning the rape of 'yet another Naga girl by a person of Bangladeshi origin in Dimapur'. With little more evidence than the girl's accusation, locals gathered at City Tower to protest the rape and demand justice for the victim. By 1pm, the crowd had grown to thousands. A large group from the crowd then marched to Dimapur Central Jail to demand the accused be handed over. At 3pm, the group overwhelmed the guards at the jail and pulled Khan out of the cells. Khan was beaten, stripped naked, had a rope tied around his waist and was then dragged seven kilometres back to City Tower. On the way, the procession stopped to allow crowd members to thrash and beat the accused. By 6pm, Khan had been killed somewhere between the jail and City Tower, and his lifeless body was dragged by rope for the final stretch of road to the tower. At the tower, vigilantes in the crowd held Khan's limp body upright for photos. In the photos Khan is unrecognizable, with the skin torn off his face from being dragged along the asphalt and dirt. Khan's body was then tied to the fence surrounding City Tower with bamboo poles pushed into his crotch and stomach to prop his body up for the crowd to see. In the days following the lynching, shops that were associated with Bengali speakers or suspected of being owned by Bangladeshis were ransacked and residents suspected of being Bangladeshi were targeted by vigilante gangs. Anybody of Bangladeshi or Bengali appearance, anybody who was Muslim, or anybody who was suspected of being Muslim was a potential target. Many shop owners in Dimapur's central area closed their shutters and fled the state. On 6 March, after Khan's body had been retrieved by police, it was confirmed that Khan was not a Bangladeshi migrant, but was a 35-year-old Assamese-born used car salesman.

The lynching of Syed Khan was an extreme example, rare in terms of its severity and viciousness, of the tensions surrounding migration in Nagaland. Similar violent episodes have occured following attacks on Naga women and girls by outsiders, though these are often on a much smaller scale. Sexual violence occurs within the Naga community as well, but attacks committed by Nagas within the Naga community are often trivialized or hushed and swept away. In these cases the blame for sexual attacks is often placed on the victim. Kikon (2015) argues that when there is a sexual attack within the Naga community, fears of shame and a tendency to excuse men for their acts, and often to blame women for inciting men, encourage a culture of impunity regarding sexual violence. When outsiders attack or are accused of attacking Naga women, it is different. Accusations that non-Nagas, in particular people from Bangladesh, are coming into the state and committing heinous crimes tap into ideas that Naga society, and other tribal societies as well, are at risk of being overwhelmed by migrants from the plains who look different, speak different languages, have different religions, different diets, and different morals. As these areas open up to further migration, motivated by opportunities presented in the wake of ceasefire, the issue of outsiders has become especially tumultuous and politically divisive.

Resistance to the IBI menace is highly gendered. While some political issues such as the state's drug and alcohol problems have been championed by women's civil society groups, particularly the Naga Mothers Association, issues related to outsiders and migration into the state have firmly fallen into the realm of men's politics, being closely associated with territory, land, and ideas of invasion. Rallies opposing outsiders settling in Nagaland, and more recent efforts to enforce a Register of Indigenous Inhabitants of Nagaland (RIIN) are overwhelmingly dominated by Naga men. Calls for the expansion of strict migration laws such as the Inner Line Permit system to Dimapur were made by male customary leaders and debated in Nagaland's all-male legislative assembly. At the village and town level, student unions and community groups lead drives to enumerate and expel illegal immigrants from towns and villages with the assistance of all-male Naga customary leaders such as Gaonburas and Dobashis. Riots and demonstrations in the wake of IBI-suspected sexual attacks are typically crowded with men of various ages. Women attend protests and demonstrations as well, although in much smaller numbers. Vandalism and ransacking of shop suspected to belong to Bangladeshis and non-locals occurs at times of heightened Naga/non-Naga tension, and is almost exclusively carried out by groups of Naga men. Violence targeting outsiders also extends to members of the Naga community. Naga women who have relationships with or are suspected to have relationships with non-Nagas are especially at risk of being ostracized, shamed, and even violently attacked by other Nagas. As recently as 2019, Nagaland's Chief Minister Neiphiu Rio raised the possibility of stripping Naga women of their tribal status if they marry non-Nagas (Karmakar, 2019). In other words, while Nagaland's opening up has encouraged mutually beneficial entanglements between Nagaland and India in terms of economies, politics, and even personal relationships, simultaneously outsiders are looked upon with great suspicion, and violence against outsiders is common and widespread. The idea of the IBI menace is central to all of this.

In this chapter, I consider the ways that the IBI menace has become a fundamental issue in debates about gender, identity, and men's roles in Naga society in the wake of ceasefire. I make two arguments. First, I argue that as Nagaland undergoes immense and often difficult-to-predict changes, resistance to outsiders has become a highly gendered practice that offers Naga men a means to reassert legitimacy as guardians and protectors of Naga territory, culture, and society. Second, I argue that the influx of outsiders has provided a means for men in Nagaland to place responsibility for social issues that have either emerged or become more prominent in the two decades since ceasefire onto non-Nagas. To make these arguments, I first introduce and detail Nagaland's 'IBI menace' in light of a wider 'outsiders discourse' in Northeast India, and in light of observations, discussions, and interviews held in Nagaland between January 2016 and January 2020. Second, I describe the ways the IBI menace has become a symbol of invasion and an impetus for the assertion and continued support for men's roles in Nagaland as guardians and protectors of Naga territory, culture, and society from outside intruders. Finally, I discuss the ways the IBI menace is utilized to justify surveillance and control of Naga women.

Sexual Politics and the IBI Menace

It's these Miyas, they come in for the land. These Naga girls, from village, they're naïve, they don't know anything. Then slowly, slowly, he works his way in. Then as soon as marriage, he takes everything, everything he can get. Then what can she do? He will take over before she even knows what's happened.[1]

Gabriel interrupted himself to relight his biri cigarette, furiously struggling with the lighter as he did, his shaky hands were a result of years of drinking adulterated alcohol that had, as Gabriel described it, damaged his nervous system. I had known Gabriel for two years, in which time significant changes had taken place in his life. When I first met Gabriel, he was approaching 40 years old, had found a secure government job, and after a period of regular and heavy drinking had recently completed a stay in a rehabilitation facility. Now, Gabriel appeared to be in a much better situation. While his hands still shook and he had problems with fine motor skills such as using a lighter, as many recovering alcoholics do, he was focused on work, had lost a noticeable amount of weight, and by his own account had managed to stay sober for almost three years. I asked whether Gabriel had thought about getting married in the near future. Gabriel had been struggling with this 'next step', however. Gabriel was in his forties, and many of his friends and peers married at much younger ages. Women in Gabriel's age group had already been 'married off', and, as such, Gabriel's prospects were growing dimmer. As we discussed the complex politics of marriage in Nagaland, Gabriel grew agitated. He talked about outsiders coming into the state, and surmised that it is harder for Naga men to marry Naga women now because Miyas are taking over the economy, taking work away from Naga men, and through deceitful methods of seduction were marrying their way into the Naga community in large numbers in order to take over the state. We had

1   Interview (January 2018)

not started our discussion on the topic of Miyas in Nagaland, or people of darker and typically Bengali appearance. However, Gabriel's sudden pivot to the topic of outsiders and migrants was not a surprise. I had heard similar assertions before, during fieldwork in 2016 and while travelling in Nagaland's isolated eastern districts in 2012. Discussions of the IBI menace often began with concerns about changing demography and the overwhelming numbers of people in the surrounding plains who may migrate into Nagaland, but then quickly turned to the issues of IBI men. IBI men were portrayed as destitute, dirty, and underhanded in their business dealings.

Bangladesh and the illegal Bangladeshi migrant (IBI) are central to the outsiders discourse. Bangladesh is associated with overpopulation, landlessness, and extreme poverty. The IBI menace is a highly gendered construction, almost always spoken about in terms of a Bengali speaking male, that has gained relevance in Nagaland since ceasefires were signed and since the state has liberalized and opened up. Outsiders are perceived to be coming into the state, marrying and having children with Naga women and this has magnified fears that Nagas will be 'bred out' and become a minority in their own state. There is a popular perception among many Northeast Indian tribal communities that hordes of Bangladeshi migrants are spilling across India's porous border into Northeast India in search of jobs, land, and livelihoods. The IBI menace represents a collection of ideas about migrants in Nagaland, many of which are contradictory but are nonetheless greatly influential in terms of resistance to Bangladeshi migrants and suspected Bangladeshi migrants. The imagined IBI is unemployed, uneducated, and destitute, but is also stealing jobs from Nagas, is cunning, and is attempting to take-over Nagaland. The imagined IBI is an unhygienic sexual deviant and a rapist, but is also charming and seducing his way into the Naga community. The nearby state of Tripura, bordered on three sides by Bangladesh, is often mentioned in discussions of the IBI menace as a place where this has happened. Tripura is popularly discussed, in Tripura itself and in other states of India, as having been taken over by migrants from Bangladesh and the offspring of migrants from Bangladesh. In tribal states throughout Northeast India, Tripura is used as an illustration of a 'worst case' scenario where tribal communities have been relegated to a minority in their homeland by hordes of Bangladeshi migrants (Deb and Mahato, 2017). Politicians in other states in Northeast India evoke Tripura to justify resistance to outsiders, and evoke fears of infiltration and invasion (Ghoshal, 2019). Below, my discussion with 'Mark', a Naga shopkeeper in Dimapur is illustrative of the ways the IBI menace permeates into any discussions of outsiders, land, and gender in Nagaland.

'Like Tripura'

Mark and I sat in his shop in Dimapur in late 2017. I had been conducting follow-up interviews with shopkeepers in the area that I had spoken with in early 2016. I mentioned to Mark that in a number of other shops, I noticed more Bihari and Bengali workers than I had seen on earlier visits. Mark was quick to point out that I could not know if they were Bihari, Bengali, or if they were Bangladeshi migrants. He emphasized that recently more migrants had come into Dimapur from Bangladesh and that parts of the city are completely dominated by Bangladeshi migrants. Mark's suspicions were somewhat valid. There is a population of Bangladeshi migrants in Nagaland, and Dimapur especially. However, the part of town I assumed he was referring to, 'Marwari Patti' and the 'New Market' area, were dominated, as the name suggests, by Marwari traders, a migrant population that has roots in the Indian state of Rajasthan, many of whom have been in Dimapur since the late 19th century. There is a large Muslim community in the area, with four mosques in the immediate area. Many residents and shopkeepers in Marwari Patti speak Bengali, but also Bhojpuri, Magahi, Maithili, and Hindi. Because of this, Marwari Patti, the New Market area, and the neighbourhoods to the south of Marwari Patti are often thought to house a significant number of IBIs. Traders in Marwari Patti are often suspected to be IBIs and shops and businesses in Marwari Patti are often vandalized at times of heightened ethnic tension. Mark and I discussed the IBI population in Marwari Patti, and the tensions surrounding IBIs in Nagaland. I brought up the 5 March 2015 lynching as an example of responses to IBIs, knowing that Mark witnessed the crowd at City Tower on the day of the lynching. Mark summarized the anxieties surrounding the IBI menace while describing the riot and the motivations for the riot:

> (If he was a Naga man, would it have been the same?)
> No, it wouldn't have been the same. Wouldn't be the same. Just because he was an outsider, and an outsider doing something to a woman like this, was not good. That's what the people thought. They [IBIs] enter, now slowly outsider is enter ... Nagas are alert. They know what's going on now. They're conscious about this migration. But they still get the land. All over Dimapur, all Miyas [people of Bengali and Bangladeshi appearance] own. And then they're everywhere. These Bangladeshis have seven, eight, ten children, then more, then more. It's always growing. More coming ... Before now, we never even had this problem. Rapes were very rare, sometimes, sometimes, but very rare, almost none. It will be like a Tripura. Look at

Tripura, sad condition. And then, at that time, everything got exploded. Everybody, men, women, everybody got crazy ... Tripura, is, the local people are like tribes, ok like us, Tripura, but actually the President, Chief Minister, is ruled by Bangladesh. It's a very sad thing.

Mark's assertions that it was impossible to know whether Biharis or Bengalis were in fact IBIs was a caution commonly shared. Illegal migrants are believed to counterfeit or otherwise procure Indian birth certificates and other documentation with ease. Because of this, and because of the difficulties distinguishing Assamese, Bihari, Bengali and Bangladeshi migrants, the term IBI is applied to a much larger population of non-Nagas than just illegal Bangladeshi migrants. Anybody who may be Muslim, may speak Bengali, or is darker skinned is associated with the IBI menace, and is placed under the IBI category. Likewise, the appearance of new mosques, as well as Hindu temples and shrines, such as those in the Marwari Patti area, is often referenced as one barometer for the influx of IBIs into Nagaland and their growing influence in the state. Resistance to this growing influence is predictably politicized and is influenced by Naga elites and used by elites to pursue their own political ends. Sexual politics surrounding the IBI is particularly volatile. The IBI is imagined simultaneously as a sexually deviant rapist, and as a charming provocateur who tricks and seduces Naga women as a means of 'marrying into' the Naga community.

There was a widely shared perception that male IBIs were coming to Nagaland in order to take ownership of land in the state. Strictly speaking, outsiders cannot buy land in Nagaland. However, outsiders do, some of whom have come from Bangladesh. This is thought to be done either through paying or otherwise colluding with Naga intermediaries, or through marrying Naga women and either taking on Naga names through marriage or having children and giving those children Naga names (Manchanda and Kakran, 2017: 74). The general consensus was that migrants, specifically Bangladeshi migrants, were coming into Nagaland in large numbers, and charming and seducing Naga women so as to marry their way into the Naga community and own land in the state. Words such as 'cunning' and 'trickster' were often used to describe IBIs or Miya/Naga relationships. Bengali and Bangladeshi women were rarely brought up in discussions about the IBI menace, except where their ability to produce large numbers of the children of IBI men is referenced. Naga men's relationships with Bengali and Bangladeshi women were also given much less scrutiny in discussions of the IBI menace, and Naga men who did marry women outside of the Naga community were rarely mentioned. This was not due to Naga men marrying women of Bangladeshi or Bengali heritage being rare. Naga men also marry non-Nagas, including women of Bangladeshi or Bihari heritage. Rather, the issue of concern was that Naga women would lose their Naga heritage when marring a non-Naga, reflecting an ideology that when Naga women marry, they adopt the identity of their husband and surrender their own cultural heritage. This resistance, however, does not only target IBIs and other outsiders. Concerns that Naga women are engaging with non-Nagas has stoked concentrated efforts to monitor and intervene in the movements and relationships of Naga women to discourage intermarriages with outsiders and the 'breeding out' of Naga society. This was recently raised during a speech by Nagaland's Chief Minister, Neiphiu Rio on 12 January 2019. Rio addressed a crowd at Loyem Memorial, in Tuensang, one of Nagaland's more isolated districts, to clarify the Government of Nagaland's position on the Citizenship Amendment Bill 2016. During the speech, Chief Minister Rio made special note of public interest in measures to confiscate Naga women of their tribal status if they marry non-Nagas, effectively rescinding their identities as Naga. Essentially, protecting Naga society involves increasing surveillance and intervention in the movements and relationships of Naga women, under threat of their identities as Nagas being forfeited if they marry an outsider, more specifically, an IBI or suspected IBI.

While the Chief Minister's comment about Naga women's tribal status being forfeited if they marry outside of the Naga community was brief, the context it appeared in is illustrative of the ways Naga women's relationships with outsiders, and particularly with IBIs and people suspected to be IBIs, are framed. Rio's speech sought to allay anxieties surrounding a bill that may allow non-locals to settle in Nagaland in greater numbers. Similar bills have been considered in Nagaland's neighbouring tribal states. In August and September 2019 in Mizoram, the Mizo student union, Mizo Zirlai Pawl (MZP) led an awareness campaign in Mizoram's schools and colleges warning of the impacts of Mizo/non-Mizo unions and dissuading Mizo women from marrying non-Mizo men (Chakraborty, 2008). Likewise, in the state of Meghalaya pushes to debar Khasi women of their tribal status if they marry outsiders and to refute tribal status to children of those unions have enjoyed popular support since the 1970s, most recently in the form of the Khasi Hills Autonomous District (Khasi Social Custom of Lineage) Second Amendment Bill (2018) (Chhakchhuak, 2019). These Bills and similar legislative attempts at debarring tribal women of their tribal identities as a punishment for their involvement with non-tribal men rarely, if ever, pass. However, the enduring support for these laws among a significant number of people in Nagaland is informed by a wider discourse outsiders, women, and identity. Naga women who marry or have relationships with

men outside the Naga community are perceived to be traitors and threats
to the survival of Naga society, and are often ostracized from their villages
and families (Kikon, 2015).

Conclusion

Resisting outsiders in Nagaland is entangled in a masculine discourse that
frames Naga men as protectors Naga territory, culture and society from
outside encroachments, and Naga women as victims of encroachment, as
lacking agency, and in need of protection through close surveillance and
control over their movements and relationships. Grassroots movements that
focus on the IBI menace were and are overwhelmingly attended by men, and
often involve a discourse that frames IBIs as a risk for Naga women, and Naga
men as guarding against and resisting that risk. Similar politics have been
identified and discussed in other contexts, often also involving outsiders
coming into tribal majority states, and often involving Bangladeshi migrants
in particular coming into tribal majority states. In Meghalaya, McDuie-Ra
(2006, 2007) identifies an outsiders discourse where the issue of migration and
resisting migrants dominates social and political life and is co-opted by civil
society actors and political actors into a vast array of issues and insecurities.
Where a cause of insecurity can be politicized in terms of the outsiders
discourse, it is contested, debated, and addressed by the state and civil society
actors. Where a cause of insecurity is not politicized in terms of the outsiders
discourse, it is marginalized or co-opted into the outsiders discourse as a
problem itself (McDuie-Ra, 2007: 371). Likewise Chakraborty (2008) details an
emerging gendered politics of othering in the state of Mizoram in Northeast
India, where Mizo women, as marginal members of a patriarchal Mizo
society, have found new forms of empowerment by opposing and policing
non-Mizos and outsiders in order to justify their role in constructing and
defending 'ideal Zo Christian state' (2008: 34). The IBI menace in Nagaland
is an outsiders discourse, invoking ideas of an invasion of outsiders and the
need to protect Nagaland from these invaders by emphasizing rigid gender
roles in Naga society and surveillance and control over the movements and
relationships of Naga women. In Nagaland specifically, the IBI menace is a
means to politicize women's bodies in a context where women are becoming
more liberated and the rigidly gendered ideas that underpin Naga patriarchy
are increasingly being challenged. The debate about outsiders in Nagaland
has become co-opted with the gendered debate. Migrants are opposed and
resisted in various ways. Many of these ways involve male leadership and

are dominated by men. The discussion of outsiders taking over Nagaland has become closely entwined with the question of women's agency in Nagaland. The IBI menace thus informs a politics of closer surveillance and control of Naga women's relationships, with threats of ostracism and the loss of tribal identity for transgressing tribal/non-tribal lines.

References

Chakraborty, A.S. (2008). 'Emergence of women from "private" to "public": A narrative of power politics from Mizoram'. *Journal of International Women's Studies* 9(3): 27–45.

Chhakchhuak, L. (2019). 'Why are Khasi women being held responsible for the "dilution" of the Tribe?' Available at: https://www.jaijagat2020.org/post/why-are-khasi-women-being-held-responsible-for-the-dilution-of-the-tribe?fb_comment_id=1446812105431156_1448729731906060 (accessed 2 September 2019).

Deb, M.K. and Mahato, A. (2017). 'Understanding the politics around illegal migration from Bangladesh into Assam and Tripura'. *Asian Journal of Research in Social Sciences and Humanities* 7(9). 222–234. DOI: 10.5958/2249-7315.2017.00456.7.

Ghoshal, A. (2019). *Refugees, borders and identities: Rights and habitat in East and Northeast India*. New York, 200–244.

Karmakar, S. (2019). 'Nagaland mulls law to check marriage to non-Nagas'. Guwahati. Available at: https://www.deccanherald.com/national/nagaland-mulls-law-check-712850.html (accessed 21 August 2019).

Kikon, D. (2015). *Life and dignity: Women's testimonies of sexual violence in Dimapur (Nagaland)*. Guwahati: North Eastern Social Research Centre.

Laskar, N.I. (2015). 'Dimapur lynching: The Nagaland picture has cracked'. *The Citizen*, 11 March.

Manchanda, R. and Kakran, S. (2017). 'Gendered power transformations in India's Northeast: Peace politics in Nagaland'. *Cultural Dynamics* 29(1): 63–82. DOI: 10.1177/0921374017709232.

McDuie-Ra, D. (2006). 'Civil society organisations and human security: Transcending constricted space in Meghalaya'. *Contemporary South Asia* 15(1): 35–53. DOI: 10.1080/09584930600938040.

McDuie-Ra, D. (2007). 'The constraints on civil society beyond the state: Gender-based insecurity in Meghalaya, India'. *Voluntas* 18: 359–384. DOI: 10.1007/s11266-007-9047-3.

Nagaland Post (2019). 'AYO holds discourse on social issues'. 18 May. Dimapur.

Thyrniang, A. (2015) 'Dimapur horror – An unjustifiable crime'. *The Shillong Times*, 10 March. Shillong.

Closing

Abstract

I conclude this book with a reflection on the ways Nagaland exemplifies the making and unmaking of borders – cartographic, legal, and cultural – and the ways this ongoing process creates new forms of liberation and marginalization that inform critical approaches to gender, place, and identity.

Keywords: borderlands, anxiety, gender

Nagaland exemplifies a contemporary borderland emerging from decades of armed conflict. The state shares an extended and porous border with Burma, as well as borders with the neighbouring Indian states of Arunachal Pradesh, Assam and Manipur. These borders are contested, often violently, by state governments attempting wrestle control of valuable resource pools and border communities. Nagaland's borders are also contested by non-state actors within Nagaland who reject the state's 1963 map entirely in favour of an alternative map, 'Nagalim', which includes territory in surrounding states and across the international border with Myanmar. Since India's Independence in 1947, Nagaland has been mired in conflict between the Government of India and Naga nationalist groups agitating for various forms of autonomy and sovereignty. This conflict is rooted in histories of difference and distance to the Indian state centre, and like conflicts in many other borderlands, involved a protracted and draconian state response marked by militarization, exceptional laws, and targeting suspect populations for perceived subversion and resistance. Throughout this conflict, Naga nationalist groups divided along ideological and tribal lines into competing factions, and targeted the Naga public in paranoid efforts to weed out suspected spies and traitors, and predatory efforts to extort money, food and shelter. Since ceasefires were signed in the late 1990s and early 2000s between the Government of India and two of the largest Naga nationalist factions, the borderland state has hosted a tense peace-conflict continuum. This tense peace is marked by a

Wilkinson, Matthew: *Borderland Anxieties. Shifting Understandings of Gender, Place and Identity at the India-Burma Border.* Amsterdam: Amsterdam University Press, 2023
DOI: 10.5117/9789463729789_CLOS

layered and complex milieu of sovereign actors, including the Nagaland state government and various Naga nationalist groups, a parallel militarized state that exists above and outside of state law, and local customary institutions enshrined and protected under Indian Constitutional law. As Nagaland's decades of conflict are being brought to a close, changes are taking place in the state that reflect changes taking place in other South and Southeast Asian borderlands.

Post-conflict changes in Nagaland offer a window to understanding how politics, gender and anxiety intersect in a borderland state experiencing rapid social, political, and economic developments. New connections to and accelerated flows with India are a stark contrast to previous experiences of militarization and forced displacement. Naga communities are becoming more connected to India, and India is being experienced and understood in ways that are more associated with economic opportunity and political inclusion. There are numerous interruptions, setbacks, and exceptions to this phenomenon, however, life in Nagaland is nevertheless more entangled and attached to India than ever before, and in more ways than ever before. Accelerating flows and stronger connections take place alongside ongoing militarization, nationalist insurgency, and debates about the locations, porosity and legitimacy of the state's borders. In light of these new engagements, the Naga nationalist vision offered by Phizo and the Naga National Council in the 1940s and 1950s, a complex marriage of tribal customs and institutions, Socialist ethics, and rigidly gendered interpretations of Christian morality, is less relevant and less attractive for many. The Naga nationalist workers that embody and represent the nationalist push are more often encountered as extortionists and criminals, and the leadership of many nationalist groups are perceived to live opulent lifestyles funded by illegal taxes and forced donations. Nationalist workers and fighters who leave often find themselves living at the margins of a post-conflict economy that has little need for professional fighters, and a post-conflict society that has experienced decades of violence and predation at the hands of nationalist workers and fighters.

Where Naga nationalism has not delivered the village-based tribal utopia it once promised, engagements with India are marked by new commercial infrastructure, employment opportunities, and new consumer goods and services in a borderland state that has, until recently, had very few of these things. For an emerging post-conflict middle class especially, these engagements encourage a reordering of aspirations, away from fulfilling rigidly gendered customs and norms tied to village life, and towards engaging in a global, consumption-based culture that offers opportunities

and possibilities previously only available to a small population of established elites. Liberalization is also marginalizing. Older men especially,
a population typically considered to be empowered through Nagaland's
patriarchal customary institutions and 'strongman' political culture,
have been excluded from many of the changes taking place in Nagaland
in the post-conflict era due to their age and their lack of marketable skills.
However, changes taking place in the state emerging from ceasefire and
liberalization, also provide new avenues for men, especially conservative
men and elites, to affirm conflict-informed masculine norms that portray
men as guardians of Naga territory, culture, and society. These affirma-
tions are rooted in two post-conflict developments. First, as Naga women
especially have become more economically empowered and independent,
and increasingly demand representation and access to decision-making
bodies and rights to inherit ancestral land, critical voices within the Naga
community question and challenge many of the rigidly gendered customs
and structures that govern life in the state. Calls for equal access and
women's representation in state politics, customary institutions and for
the rights to inherit and own ancestral lands are framed by conservative
voices as an internal threat to customs and institutions that dictate a rigidly
gendered social order as a bedrock of Naga society. Second, an influx of
migrants into the state, encouraged by the state's newfound stability and
the growth of the post-conflict economy has become a symbol of invasion and incursion of populations of outsiders into Nagaland. Outsiders,
popularly perceived to be from Bangladesh and often referred to as the
'IBI menace', are framed as a demographic threat to Naga society, one that,
if unchecked, will grow in the state until Nagas are a minority in their
own homeland. The IBI menace is a complex amalgamation of anxieties,
encompassing fears of a horde of migrants coming into the state, but
also of crime and especially sexual crime committed by migrants, and
simultaneously of migrants marrying into the Naga community through
various forms of trickery. While maintaining colonial bordering policies
such as the Inner Line Permit system offers some protection from the IBI
menace, perceptions of state dysfunction allowing migrants to come into
the state continue.

The effect of these assertions is a justification by Naga elites and conservatives for the continued enforcement of rigid gender roles and the
uncompromising maintenance of traditional customary institutions. Any
threat, perceived threat, or potential threat to these gender roles or to
these customary institutions is interpreted as a threat to the foundations
and survival of Naga society. In some ways, ideas of 'equality as tradition'

in the form of rigid and natural gender roles are emphasized by Nagaland's post-conflict opening up greater engagement with India. These roles have become symbolic markers of a distinct Naga identity, and their survival is, for many Nagas, associated with the survival of Naga identity amid social, cultural, and political changes. In other words, two decades of ceasefire has not made conflict-informed masculine norms redundant, but has provided new arenas for conflict-informed masculine norms to appear in. This is a crucial contribution to understandings of anxiety, gender and change in complex political landscapes such as borderlands and other sites emerging from conflict.

Reflecting on what has been an immense research journey, one that has involved numerous trips to a welcoming and beautiful but contested and often violent part of the world, some closing and final remarks and clarifications need to be made. These remarks and clarifications serve as my way of, somewhat apologetically, thanking and crediting countless people in Nagaland who, over years, aided me in understanding life in a place that is very different to where I am from and showed immense care, tolerance, and patience. First, this book is in no way an attempt to critique or criticize men in Nagaland. The purpose of this book was not to chastise or shame men in Nagaland who oppose women's political involvement, men such as those who took part in the 2017 Urban Local Body election riots, or the men who expressed reservations about women's property rights in Nagaland, women's sexual agency, or feminist and inclusive ideas about citizenship. Rather, in this book, I have attempted to show how Nagaland's patriarchal backlash is shaped in a context of immense and rapid social, political and economic changes, ongoing insecurities, and ideologies that place women's political involvement and Naga identity as at-odds with each other. Ongoing support for patriarchal institutions in Nagaland is not a matter of conservative men and elites safeguarding their own social empowerment. It is a matter of conflicting ideologies and anxieties in a contested and insecure frontier. In the years I have been visiting Nagaland, I have been fortunate to meet and spend time with welcoming, insightful, and intelligent men. Some of the men discussed in this book have brought me into their homes and families, have trusted me to hear and tell their stories, and on several occasions have shared secrets with me that could put them at great risk. Many of the men I spoke to have had extremely violent histories, and their openness and willingness to sit with me, share, and reflect is telling of the complexities that living in a contested borderland involves.

Second, this book has from its outset attempted to show and discuss how men in Nagaland experience ceasefire, and the changes that have come with ceasefire. This is a very difficult thing to do. Ceasefire has shaped people's lives in Nagaland in myriad ways, which are often difficult to ascribe directly to ceasefire and its changes. The ongoing support for Naga autonomy in Nagaland suggests that, to a degree, resistance to India has never really ended. Overall though, for men in Nagaland ceasefire means that joining a Naga nationalist group, going 'underground', and taking part in armed conflict is a less realistic livelihood option, and the economic and social changes that ceasefire has brought to Nagaland has brought jobs and livelihood options into Nagaland that are greatly beneficial. Conflict has not entirely ended, but people living in Nagaland today are less likely to be killed or maimed in conflict than before ceasefire and have greater agency in their lives than during the conflict as well. Some men who became close friends of mine during this research are denied many of the benefits of the changes in the state and find themselves at the margins of Nagaland's post-conflict economy and society. It is difficult to say if these men would have been better off had ceasefires never been signed at all, but it is doubtful. Overall, and despite the gendered insecurities and emerging forms of conflict discussed in this book, life for men and for women in Nagaland has improved as a result of ceasefire.

Finally, this book has called for a wider consideration and more nuanced discussion of masculinities in the wake of conflict and during ceasefire. As I have discussed throughout, conflict shapes understandings of masculinity – the thoughts, actions, and behaviours associated with men. These understandings often associate hegemonic forms of masculinity with involvement in conflict, violence, warlordism, and strongman politics. This is very visible in Nagaland, where conflict has contributed to the maintenance of and has arguably magnified a rigidly gendered social order where men are guardians and protectors of Naga territory, culture, and society, and where women are non-political subjects in need of protection. However, throughout this book I have also shown that the closing of conflict at the borderland allows voices to emerge that question and challenge these rigidly drawn understandings of Naga society. New discussions and debates are taking place, and in light of these discussions and debates, change is occurring in the public and private sphere. This change is slow and is marked by ongoing tensions and resistance, but it is occurring, nonetheless. Ongoing debates about gender and discussions about how a society works after decades of conflict suggests that even prolonged, interrupted, and stalled peacebuilding efforts, as is the case in Nagaland, represent critical points of reflection and opportunities for change in societies marked by conflict. Arguably, the anxieties associated with borderlands magnify these tensions and this change, justifying further attention on borderlands as sites of meaning-making. Future research on gender, conflict, and borderlands must continue these nuanced discussions and debates at the local level, as crucial moments of change that do not only take place between conflict actors, but take place on streets, in people's homes, in churches, and in everyday interactions that are easily overlooked.

Index